Cake
DECORATIONS

BASIC CAKES
PAINTING WITH CHOCOLATE
FIGURINES IN FONDANT

Lannoo

My fascination with baking started in my early childhood. As a little girl I was very creative, always busy with pencil and paper. Even at school I followed a creative route and that's how I ended up in the graphics sector. When I graduated, my brother had just started his own bakery and there I developed my passion to combine my creative side with pastries. My brother and his wife baked, my mom ran the shop and my dad got his degree as ice cream maker. We are therefore a family business par excellence. The first orders quickly came in through word of mouth. Photos were taken of my cakes. Thereafter I started my Facebook page 'Taarten Tatyana'. I soon discovered my strongest point in the world of cake design: sculpting edible figures. Over the years, my figures have become more refined and detailed.

It has been ten years since the start and I can proudly say that based on the number of followers on Facebook I am the best-known cake designer in Belgium. But most of all, in those ten years, I got to meet a lot of loyal and delightful customers who come back every year and for whom I have become a regular ritual in their lives. Because these customers encouraged me, I took the plunge and approached Uitgeverij Lannoo to co-publish this book.

In this book I would like to teach you the basic principles of a theme cake (cake covered with fondant), but especially focus on the hand-sculpted figurines. So this is not a typical baking book but rather a guide to making your cake even more fun with decorations and figures. Everything will be explained step by step, so that both a hobby baker and a professional baker can get started with this book. I would also like to emphasize that an edible figurine does not only find its place on a cake covered with fondant. You can also make the cake of your choice at home and then finish it by placing a hand-sculpted figure on it.

Let's connect!

🏀 www.taartentatyana.com

Would you like to see more of my work or do you want to share your baking and figurine creations with me? Add and tag me on social media!

f taartentatyana

📷 #taartentatyana

♪ @taartentatyana

CONTENT

CHAPTER 1
Themed cakes

Themed cakes	10
Layer cakes	16
Modeling basics	24

CHAPTER 2
Basic figures

Rose	32
Half a football	33
Pine tree	34
Bow	35
Crown	36
Unicorn horn	37

CHAPTER 3
Animals

Pig	40
Frog	42
Fox	44
Lion	46
Owl	50
Dog	53
Cat	56
Panda	60
Fish	63
Penguin	66

CHAPTER 4
Well-known characters

Bumba	70
Unicorn	73
Fat unicorn	76
Smurf	80
Dinosaur	84
Baby	88
Pardoes	92

CHAPTER 5
Food cartoons

Rainbow	100
Ice lolly	102
Raspberry	104
Blueberry	106
Chocolate candy	107
Apple	108
Watermelon	110
Pear	112
Cherries	114
Orange	116
Donut	118
Hamburger	120
Cupcake	122

CHAPTER 6
Festive occasions

Giant cupcake	126
Christmas	130
Easter	137
Halloween	142
Valentines	150
Mother's day	152
Communion	156

chapter 01

THEMED CAKES

Themed cakes

You can make a themed cake in different ways. In doing so you will discover what suits you best. We'll start with the basics first.

A themed cake is usually made with sponge cake. The outside of the cake can be quite heavy and that is why it is important to keep the inside as light as possible. The extra filling you put between your sponge layers is up to you. We prefer to keep this filling simple as well. After the cake is baked, we use sugar water to make sure the cake doesn't get dry inside. Then we will mask the outside with butter or ganache and finally, the fondant goes on top. There are many different ways to bake, fill and mask a themed cake, but in this book I want to show you the way I always do it.

We start with the sponge cake

BASIC RECIPES

SPONGE CAKE

6 eggs
200 g (7 oz) granulated sugar
40 g (1½ oz) good-quality butter
200 g (7 oz) flour
1 tsp baking powder
1 dash of vanilla extract
a pinch of salt

PREPARATION
Preheat the oven to 180°C (356°F). Beat the eggs lightly and then add the granulated sugar. Beat for a while until you have an airy foamy mass. Melt the butter and add this to the egg mixture. Keep mixing. Mix the flour with the baking powder and sift it gently into the batter. Then add the vanilla extract and salt.
Grease a 23 cm diameter and 6 cm high springform pan with a little butter. Pour the batter into the springform pan and set it in the oven for 40 minutes. Remove it from oven and let it cool.

. *tip* .

Would you like to make cupcakes? Then use this same recipe! Many people go for a Madeira or pound cake recipe when they make cupcakes, but in combination with the fondant or other decorations this quickly becomes too heavy. Sponge cake always stays light and is therefore also perfect for cupcakes or cake pops!

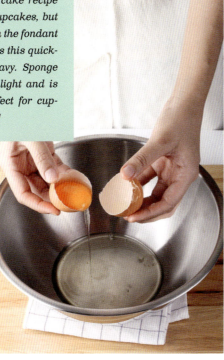

BASIC RECIPES

SUGAR WATER

175 g (6 oz) granulated sugar
100 g (3½ oz) water

PREPARATION
Mix the sugar with the water and let it boil to 100°C (212°F). Stir the mixture well and let it cool.

. tip .
You can easily keep sugar water for months in your fridge.

BUTTERCREAM

262 ml (0.55 pints/0.28 quarts) water
600 g (21.16 oz) sugar
37.5 g (1.32 oz) glucose
6 eggs
375 g (13.23 oz) good-quality butter
375 g (13.23 oz) margarine

PREPARATION
Mix the water, sugar and glucose and let it boil until 121°C (250°F). Gently beat the mixture together with the eggs. Beat the mixture when lukewarm, then add the butter and the margarine and beat until the consistency of the buttercream becomes firm.

Note:
Recipe for a whole bucket/multiple cakes. Divide by 4 if it is for 1 big cake only.

. tip .
You can store buttercream in the fridge for a week. This will make it hard. When you want to use it again, heat it for a little less than a 1 minute in the microwave, after which mix it well again. Buttercream separates very quickly. By beating well - and possibly heating a little extra depending on your amount - it becomes usable again. Make sure to beat it thoroughly: when your buttercream is too runny, it is difficult to mask with it.

BASIC RECIPES

GANACHE

200 ml (7 fl oz) milk
10 g (0.35 oz) glucose
200 g (7 oz) dark chocolate, cut into pieces
200 g (7 oz) milk chocolate, cut into pieces
80 g (2.82 oz) butter, cut into pieces

PREPARATION
Let the milk and glucose boil and then pour this mixture onto the chocolate and butter. Stir until everything is well melted. Then let the mixture set in the refrigerator to the desired thickness. If the ganache has become too hard, heat it up again and stir well.

buttercream or ganache?

Personally, I usually prefer buttercream. This gives a creamy touch to the cake and is easy to combine whatever flavor you choose for the inside. Ganache is used more often if the outside of the cake is quite compact or with 3D cakes that need a lot of support to stay upright. Ganache becomes very firm after cooling and thus provides that extra support. The big disadvantage of ganache is the chocolate taste, while buttercream has a more neutral taste. Customers often ask whether buttercream won't be too heavy but masking only covers the outside. It is therefore not a layer of 5 cm all around, but a thin layer that is not too heavy. It is up to you to choose between buttercream or ganache, it is a personal preference.

BASIC RECIPES

ICE CREAM

The base of a themed cake can also be made out of ice cream. This is ideal for people who are not fans of cake! On the outside, a themed ice cream cake looks just like one based on cake. This variant can therefore be easily decorated with rolled fondant and fitted figures. The biggest difference between a classic themed cake and the themed ice cream cake, is that the latter has to be kept in the freezer and not in the fridge. If you want to transport the themed ice cream cake, I recommend using a freezer box for transportation.

VANILLA ICE CREAM BASED ON RAW MILK

1 vanilla pod
1½ litres (3.17 pints/1.56 quarts) raw milk (fresh from the farm)
480 g (1½ oz) sugar
240 g (8.47 oz) egg yolk
(= approx. 12 yolks)
380 g (13.40 oz) cream

PREPARATION
Cut the vanilla pod in half lengthwise and remove the seeds. Add it to the milk. Bring the milk with two thirds of the sugar to the boil.

Then whisk the egg yolks combined with the rest of the sugar.

When it starts to boil, add half of the milk to the egg mixture. Mix this well. Pour the mixture back into the rest of the milk and heat until 85°C (185°F).

When the temperature is reached, take the mixture off the heat, add the cream and let it cool as quickly as possible. Blend for a few minutes with an immersion blender to make the texture lighter.

Let the mixture rest for two hours and then pour it into an ice-cream maker.

When ready, scoop the ice cream into an ice cream tin. If necessary, first place a biscuit sheet or a piece of meringue in the bottom of the tin, before scooping in the ice cream. Smooth the top of the ice cream with a spatula and place the ice cream mold in a quick freezer (20-25 min. in summer or 30-45 min. in winter).

Carefully remove the ice cream from the mold using a pastry torch. Then put it back in the freezer until you're ready to decorate the cake. Do not keep the ice cream in the freezer for longer than three months.

> **. tip .**
>
> *You can also keep this mixture a bit longer if you keep it cool. Just never let the temperature get any higher than 6°C (42°F).*

decoration:

Fill the holes with buttercream (see recipe p. 12). Then follow method as with a normal themed cake (see p. 16). You don't need to use support sticks with the themed ice cream cake.

Layer cakes

CAKE FILLING

Once you've prepared the basic cake, you're ready to go! Cut the cake twice horizontally to create three layers. Place the three layers next to each other in the correct order. Take a coarse brush that is food safe and brush sugar water over the top two layers. Don't cover the bottom layer with sugar water, because otherwise the bottom of the cake will be too soft.

Place the bottom layer on a plate and top with a filling of your choice.

Popular fillings are:
- whipped cream with pieces of fresh strawberry (nice and fresh on hot days)
- whipped cream with jam of your choice
- whipped cream with pieces of pineapple
- whipped cream with raspberries
- whipped cream with crumbled Oreo (or other cookies; let your imagination run wild)
- fresh chocolate mousse (choose an airy chocolate mousse)

Then put the second layer on top and repeat the filling. End with the top layer. We are now ready to mask.

tip

Preferably choose a filling that is not too heavy.

The 'trap' in a theme cake is that the cake looks really nice, but doesn't taste so good because it's too heavy. Keep the inside as airy as possible.

The more classic fillings (for example whipped cream with pieces of pineapple) are still the most popular among an older crowd!

MASKING

When we talk about masking we mean evenly spreading the cake with buttercream. This ensures that your cake becomes firmer and that your fondant does not get 'cellulite'. With the buttercream we eliminate all imperfections and make the outside more compact. It won't work perfectly the first time. It takes some time and practice to master this technique. By the way, masking and covering are the hardest parts. Don't get discouraged if it doesn't work so well the first time. Practice makes perfect!

Some things you should definitely pay attention to:

1. Make sure your butter has the right consistency. It certainly shouldn't be separated or too soft, because then it will drip right off the cake. Whipping it well until it is quite firm is a must.

2. Try out what works best for you. Very often I just use a palette knife. Many people use a palette knife first and then a scraper and a turntable. Experiment and persevere when it doesn't go smoothly in the beginning.

Fun to know

Another name for rolled fondant is sugar paste.

CAKE DECORATIONS

tip

If you really want a very tight cake with a sharp 90-degree angle, put the cake in the freezer for 10 minutes after masking. This is how the buttercream becomes hard and it will make it easier to cover the cake with rolled fondant. I wouldn't recommend longer than 10 min. As the intention is that only the buttercream gets hard and not that the cake itself starts to freeze.

COATING

When your cake is masked, you are ready to cover it. The most popular way to cover it is with fondant, but other products exist, such as marzipan, chocolate… Since I always work with fondant, I will describe this method.

COATING WITH ROLLED FONDANT

Rolled fondant, also known as sugar paste, is mainly made out of sugar. There are different brands, colors and flavors of fondant. My experience is: try them out for yourself! What works great for me, might not work so well for somebody else. It also depends a lot on the method you use. I have tried several brands over the years and, in Belgium, I am happiest with two specific brands: Callebaut and Bouwhuis.

Now for the coating technique:

1. Roll out the color of your choice as thinly as possible. For this, I use a rolling machine, but you can also get started with a rolling pin and some icing sugar. The trick is to roll it as thin as possible, making sure that the fondant doesn't tear and that the cake doesn't show through when it is applied. Also don't overdo it with the icing sugar; only add some if you notice that the fondant is starting to stick. The thinner the fondant, the better it tastes afterwards.

Rolled fondant dries out in the air. So it is important to put the fondant on your cake immediately after rolling it out.

2. Take hold of the rolled fondant at the top and drape it carefully over your cake. Do this in one quick move, otherwise your fondant will tear due to gravity. You can also roll the rolled fondant over your rolling pin and then drape it over your cake.

3. Third step: take a smoother. I prefer to use a smoother with a convex side on top and a sharp edge at the bottom. First smooth the top of the cake. Then go over the front with the convex side of your smoother and make a downwards movement. Repeat this all around the cake so that the sugar paste adheres nice and tight. Now go around the edges with the sharp side of the smoother. If necessary, you can always strengthen the sharp edges by pressing them together with a second smoother. When you are satisfied, cut the excess sugar paste with a sharp knife to remove it.

4. Congratulations, you're ready to decorate!

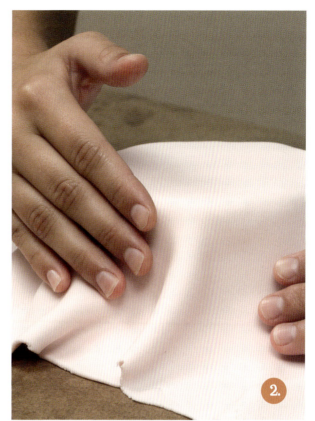

CAKE DECORATIONS

21

NAKED CAKE

If you are not an expert in coating cake with rolled fondant, then a naked cake is the ideal solution! A naked cake is a theme cake without rolled fondant. For this it is enough to make a sponge cake to mask. This too can be very beautiful and has recently become more and more fashionable. You can mix a little gel food coloring for cake with your buttercream and add some color. With a naked cake it is important to mask as tightly as possible for the best result. Naked cakes are often combined with a drip or with flowers around them to make it into a wedding cake.

CAKE DRUM

A cake drum is the plate that you put under the cake. These exist in different colors but are usually covered with rolled fondant. You can also choose not to cover it. They exist in different formats. Pick one that is bigger than your bottom layer but not too big. Think carefully about what kind of cake you have in mind and then choose the right cake drum for it. Cake drums can also be used for extra decoration, in line with your figures (see halloween cake p. 142)

TIERED CAKE

We're talking about a tiered cake when you have two or more layers on top of each other. With a tiered cake it is important to ensure good support from within. If you don't, your cake will collapse due to the weight of the top on the bottom. When supporting the cake you use cake dowels. These are available both in plastic and in wood. I always use the wooden ones because I think they are slightly more sturdy than the plastic ones. Choose whichever you find most comfortable to use.

Place a dowel in the center of the cake. Then place four more dowels towards the outer edge, as if you were marking the directions on a compass. Between the dowel stick in the middle and the outer dowels, add another extra dowel. You can choose to have only five dowel sticks instead of nine, but it's better not to take unnecessary risks and ensure good support. With very large cakes you can consider putting an extra thick dowel in the middle of the cake.

With an edible marker or knife make a mark on the middle dowel so that you know the height of the cake. Use this to cut the other dowels to the same height before placing them in the cake.

Then place a backing board on the bottom cake with the supporting dowels. I always use the gold cake boards that you can easily cut to the perfect size. Take three of these boards and stick them together with marshmallows.

Take a large bowl and put two to three marshmallows in it. Heat it for 30 sec. and paste them on the back of a cake board. Stick the next cake board to this and repeat. If your partition is not strong enough, your cake may still collapse. Following these steps you get a sturdy partition that you can adjust to the size of your cake. Now put your second cake on top and repeat the entire process as many times as it is necessary for the height of your tiered cake.

Modeling basics

WHAT DO YOU USE TO MODEL?

ROLLED FONDANT

What do you use to model? When I get this question, I always give the same answer: rolled fondant! I have also modeled with marzipan in the past and 'modeling chocolate', but I believe you can still do more with rolled fondant. It is ideal to do very fine work without it crumbling and the colors stay vivid. A lot of people mix tylose in the fondant, but if you adjust the drying times and support, this is not necessary at all. On top of that, tylose doesn't really taste pleasant.

MODELING STICKS

While modeling I use modeling sticks. Thousands of these exist in all forms and sizes. They are usually made out of plastic, but can also be made from metal or rubber. Personally I always fall back on two sticks: a pointed one and one with a spherical end. Apart from those, I often use toothpicks too. What suits me, is by definition not what suits you the best. So try and see what works best for you.

POINTED STICK   STICK WITH SPHERICAL END

HOW DO YOU START?

THE HEAD AND THE BODY

While modeling, I always start with the **head**. Then I immediately have a good benchmark for the further proportions of the figure. After shaping I usually push eye sockets into the head first. That way I get a better idea of where everything will have to be.

When the head is finished, I'll put it aside. It is now time to make the **body**. In the finished body I stick one or more sticks (usually lollipop sticks) on which I can attach the head. Working like this helps the weight of the head exert less pressure on the body and everything stays in place. With scissors you can easily cut the sticks to the desired length. Don't make them too long, because then you will be taking the risk that you will damage the head. Push the sticks into the rolled fondant immediately after finishing the body. If you only do this after your figure has dried, there is a chance of cracks.

I always let my figures **harden** for at least one day; this way you prevent your modeling work from deforming. When the body is already a little harder, it can also easily bear the weight of the head. Please note, we are modeling with sugar paste. Sugar is sensitive to moisture. So save your figures in a room that is dry and not too warm. If the place where you work is too moist, your figures will become slightly sticky, and won't harden. Also avoid direct sunlight, because this can cause the colors to fade in the long run.

. tip .

If you don't have much experience with modelling figures, then always start from a concrete example. Look at the shape of the head and try to imitate it as closely as possible. Many of my customers save my figures as souvenirs. You can do this, but take care of them by keeping them in a dry room without direct sunlight. It is difficult to say for how long you can keep the figures exactly, but a number of years is really possible. Of course it is then no longer the intention to eat them after a few weeks.

FACIAL EXPRESSIONS

With faces, expression is very important. Carefully consider which emotion you want to express and feel free to research how this emotion is usually shown.

THE BACK SIDE OF THE FIGURINE

Anyone with any experience in modeling knows that the back is the trickiest part. Yet there are different ways to finish the back beautifully as well. I am happy to share the two methods I mostly follow. The first way is to dry out your figure completely. Place the head on it, and only then start with the back. Do this by rolling fondant and blending it in nicely with the pointed modeling stick. The second method is to make a figure in Styrofoam. Then the head stays nicely round at the back and it is easier to finish the back later. If you work with Styrofoam, the figure is no longer edible and this method is not the way to go if you have a more complex figure shape. With very large figures I almost always use Styrofoam, then the whole figure weighs less. So before you start working on the figure, think about what the best option is for you regarding your specific figurine.

THE HANDS

With the hands I usually start with a ball of rolled fondant, that I mold between my fingers and then slowly flatten. Use a knife to cut the shape of the fingers. Then carefully take each finger one by one and stretch it. By rolling each finger gently, it will make it rounder and appear more realistic. Also take a good look at which hands go with which type of figure. A cartoon will often have stubbier fingers than a more realistic figure. Finally it is very important that the thumb always has a little more space around it than the other fingers. The thumb also always points to the body.

DUSTING

When you've completely finished your figure, you can choose to either dust or paint it. This is not necessary. Sometimes it doesn't give any added value to dust or paint. But if you do decide to dust/paint, make sure to buy for food-safe brushes. For dusting, there exist various loose edible powders, but there are also powders that are placed in palettes. I usually use both. Please note: while dusting you can easily spill some powder. So regularly blow away the excess powder. Another option is painting with food coloring gel. These colors are more intense than the colors from dusting. With dusting you get more the effect of shadows and blush, while with painting, the colors really change. That is why you have to consider in advance what effect you want to achieve on your figure.

BLENDING

You will see the term "blending" popping up a lot in this book. With blending I mean that you use the flat side of the round modeling stick to combine pieces of rolled fondant as if they have melted together. If you glue two pieces together, you will always see clearly the dividing line between those two pieces. By running over it with the flat side of the modeling stick, you make these two pieces seem like one whole. If you want to see how I do this, definitely watch the instructional videos on my YouTube channel!

COMBINING FIGURES TOGETHER

Just like me, you can stick small pieces of fondant together by constantly blending one piece with the other. If the piece you want to 'add' is too big and won't stay stuck, use a very small amount of water to stick the whole thing together. Do try to avoid using water. I rarely use water when sculpting. When assembling limbs I use extra sticks to attach these.

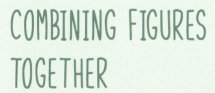

Some figures have toothpicks or pieces of steel wire in them to make or obtain a certain shape. Therefore never leave children unsupervised with the figure. Also inform your guests not to bite into a figure carelessly.

chapter 02

BASIC FIGURES

ROSE

2. For the petals, take a piece of rolled fondant in the same color and make a ball. Push this flat with both your thumbs. Make sure the top is as thin as possible. The thinner this top, the more realistic the rose will appear.

3. Now fold this petal around the teardrop. Make sure that the tip of the teardrop is always visible and does not protrude above the petals.

4. Repeat this for the next petals and fold each new petal around the teardrop at the point where you stopped with the previous petal each time. Make as many petals as you want and always make them bigger as you go.

5. The moment that you are happy with the size of your rose, cut off the bottom (I'll only do this when the rose has already been dried for a day; then you don't deform the rose while cutting). When the rose is dry you can still paint, dust it or add glitter (see p. 28)

1. Take a piece of fondant in a color of your choice and knead it until the fondant feels smooth. With your hands, shape the rolled fondant into a ball and make a teardrop of the ball. I do this by twisting my index fingers on one side, creating a sphere in between.

HALF A FOOTBALL

1. Take a plastic sphere (available at any craft store).

2. Cover it with white fondant and cut off excess edges.

3. Then roll out black fondant and take a cutter with a checked or hexagon pattern. Push the cutter firmly into the black fondant.

4. Now take one of the cut out hexagon shapes and place it in the center of the ball. Then work down until the ball is fully fitted with these hexagon shapes.

5. If desired, finish the edge by filling a piping bag with some green-colored buttercream and using the appropriate tip to create the effect of grass.

PINE TREE

1. Take a piece of rolled fondant in a green color of your choice and make a cone shape.

2. Then take a fine pair of scissors and start cutting at the bottom.

3. Continue working upwards. You get the best result if you cut somewhat irregularly, so not always the same distance between each cut.

4. Be careful not to touch the tip of the cone shape itself, or even worse to cut it off.

BOW

6. Tuck in the ends and make a few lines to make the whole look more real.

7. Optional: make two ends of the bow by cutting out two rectangles and then cutting out a small triangle at one end of each rectangle. With a little bit of water, stick them at the back of the bow.

8. Do you want the bow to look a little more rounded? Place some foil or kitchen roll between the folds in the loop of the bow and let the bow dry. Carefully remove the stuffing material when the bow has dried.

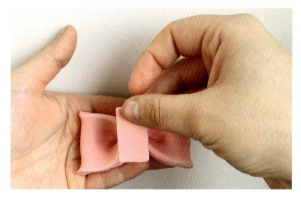

1. Roll out a piece of fondant in the color of your choice, slightly thicker than usual.

2. Cut two equal rectangles and a shorter one.

3. Take one large rectangle and hold both corners on one side. Fold these inwards.
Repeat for the other rectangle.

4. Now put the two sides together and if necessary, cut away the excess fondant in the middle.

5. Now take the small rectangle and place it vertically in the middle.

CROWN

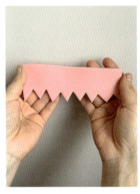

1. Roll a piece of fondant in a color of your choice, it should look a little thicker than usual. From this, cut out a long rectangle.

2. Now cut out equal triangles on one of the long sides. Do this as evenly as possible.

3. Then take a cookie cutter ring and sprinkle the outside with icing sugar, so that the crown won't stick to it. It is possible to make this without a cookie cutter ring, but then you have to roll the fondant fairly thickly.
Roll the rectangle around the cookie cutter ring. Try to make sure that the triangles at the top come out nicely. Cut smaller if necessary.

4. When you are satisfied, slightly moisten the edge of one side with water and stick it on the other side.

5. Add decoration of your choice. I have added one ball at a time. You can put a number on the crown as well. Let your fantasy run free!

6. Now let the crown dry for at least one day. Carefully remove the cookie cutter ring.

UNICORN HORN

1. Roll a piece of fondant into two long, even cones and make sure that both end in a point. Use brown fondant for gold and grey fondant for silver.

2. Now take the two cones and twist them around each other. However, the back of the horn should not get flattened. It is better to turn the horn in your hands than on a flat, hard surface.

3. Make sure they end up together in one beautiful point.

4. Then cut the back and use a skewer or lollipop stick to attach the horn to the cake at a later time.

5. Now let it dry for at least one day.

6. Spray the horn gold with a metallic spray. Optionally add edible glitter for extra effect! Do this immediately after spraying while the horn is still damp.

chapter 03
ANIMALS

ANIMALS

PIG

LEVEL OF DIFFICULTY:

1. Form the head by shaping pink fondant into a ball.

2. Push in the eye sockets with your fingers. Then narrow the upper part of the head by pushing it together.

3. With the spherical modeling stick, make the holes for the eyes and draw a line with the pointed modeling stick at the bottom of both eyes.

4. Using pink fondant, form a small ball and place this where you want the nose to be. With a toothpick you can make some lines above the nose and with the pointed modeling stick you shape the nostrils.

5. Make an opening for the mouth under the nose with the pointed modeling stick. With the flat side of the modeling stick push under the right jaw to indicate the corner of the mouth. Also indicate the location of the eyebrows.

6. To form an ear out of pink fondant, shape a triangle between your fingers. Place one side of the triangle against the head and blend it out. Now fold the top of the triangle over your pointed modeling stick. Repeat these actions for the other ear.

7. Place a ball of white fondant in each eye.

12. Form a pink ball for the body, but make it a little longer. Hold the head against it until you find the right proportion.

13. On each side of the body use a pointed modeling stick to draw one line at the bottom.

14. Push four legs into the bottom of the body with your fingers. Accentuate with the pointed modeling stick to form the curve of the belly.

15. Form small balls of white fondant and stick them on each leg. Use pink fondant to make the tail between your fingers by rolling a sausage and curling it. Place the tail on the backside of the pig.

16. Stick two sticks in the front of the body and let it dry. After drying, slide the head carefully over the sticks to attach it to the body.

CAKE DECORATIONS

8. Take the spherical modeling stick again and push the eyes in.

9. Fill the eyes and mouth with black rolled fondant.

10. Give both eyes a small white dot, to mimic some light reflection. Then for the eyebrows roll two small pieces of black rolled fondant between your fingers and bend it around the top of each eye.

11. Add extra fold lines with a toothpick and just like that, you add extra detail to your figure.

ANIMALS

FROG

LEVEL OF DIFFICULTY:

7. Create the mouth with a toothpick. Go from left to right.

8. Push the pointed modeling stick against the bottom of the mouth to make it less rigid.

9. Using green rolled fondant, make a sausage shape as long as the mouth and stick it against the bottom. Blend the corners nicely with the flat side of the modeling stick.

10. Punch two small holes in the eyes with the pointed modeling stick. Fill it with black. Also put a black line at the top of both eyes.

1. For the head and the body, shape some green fondant into an oval shape.

2. Just below the middle, you push it in with your fingers.

3. Make the top part of the head slightly pointed.

4. With your fingers push the eye sockets at the top.

5. Form two balls of white fondant and stick them on the place of the eyes. I've made one a little bit bigger than the other.

6. Place a small piece of green fondant on the top of each eye.

14. Add a front leg to both sides. Make sure that the top is narrower than the bottom.

15. Make two long sausages out of green fondant for the hind legs. Fold them in half and stick them on either side of the body.

16. Add a foot on either side as well.

17. Make the toes out of very small balls of green rolled fondant.

18. Use the toothpick to add some additional fold lines. Finally I give the frog some purple spots and a crown (see p. 36). Choose for yourself whether to do this as well. Let your imagination run wild with each figure. (Since the frog's head and body exist out of one piece, the frog does not need to dry.)

11. With the flat side of the modeling stick, push in the middle under the lip.

12. Roll out a small piece of yellow fondant and make it a semicircle. Stick this to the belly.

13. Emphasize the neck by drawing some extra lines here.

FOX

LEVEL OF DIFFICULTY:

4. Push in an eye on both sides with the spherical modeling stick. Fill this with black and make a nose as well.

5. In the middle of both the outside corners of the head, stick two small balls of white fondant for the colored sides of the fox' snout. Blend this nicely against the head.

6. Now make two ears out of orange fondant. Blend it against the head. With the flat modeling stick, make a triangle on the inside of both ears.

7. Give both eyes a small white dot to mimic light reflection.

1. Form the head out of a ball shaped piece of orange fondant, but stretch it a little more lengthwise.

2. With the spherical modeling stick, push both eye sockets in: like a kind of droplet with the narrow side facing downwards.

3. Fill both of these with white rolled fondant. Use the flat side of the pointed modeling stick to push the white in well.

8. For the body, form a blunt cone of orange fondant and a flat long droplet-shaped piece that will be the tail.

9. Wrap the tail around the bottom of the body. Create a slight curl in the tip of the tail to make it look a bit more elegant.

10. Cover the tip of the tail with white rolled fondant and blend it out nicely. Using the pointed modeling stick or a toothpick, make different lines in the tail. Make this as smooth as possible.

11. Stick two sticks into the body and let it dry. After drying, carefully slide the head over the sticks.

LION

LEVEL OF DIFFICULTY:

1. Form a ball out of yellow fondant for the head.

2. Push in the eye sockets with your fingers and with a toothpick make some pleating lines above the position of the nose.

3. Make two smaller balls of yellow fondant and stick them where the nose should go.

4. Form a small ball and push it under the two smaller balls. With the spherical modeling stick push in the middle to accentuate the mouth.

5. With the spherical modeling stick, push an eye on both sides. Create the eyebrows on each side of the face using the pointed modeling stick.

6. Fill the eyes with black rolled fondant and place a pink triangle on the two very small yellow balls.

7. Pierce each yellow ball with a toothpick to create some holes, this to suggest the whiskers.

8. Use a toothpick to draw a line under the outsides of both eyes.

9. Add the eyebrows with black.

10. Form two small yellow triangles for the ears and blend them nicely with the pointed modeling stick against the head.

11. Place a small pink triangle inside each ear to create the inside of the ear.

17. For the body, form a cone-like shape out of yellow fondant.

18. Using the blunt side of your knife, make three lines in the bottom of the cone: one in the middle and two that slant to the outsides.

19. Push the two outer lines a little deeper, with your fingers.

20. If necessary, go over the lines again with the pointed modeling stick to make them less sharp.

21. Add a piece of fondant to the bottom of each front leg. Using a toothpick, blend these into the legs to create the lion's toes.

22. Now add the hind legs. Make sure they are deeper than the two front legs lying down. If necessary, push the legs a little more backwards.

23. Form small balls of brown fondant and make the foot pads on the hind legs.

12. Now again, form a ball, this time out of brown or black fondant. This will be the lion's mane.

13. Flatten it with your fingers or roll it with your rolling pin until you have a nice round circle. Make sure it is larger than the head of the lion.

14. Use a knife to make cuts on the outside of the circle, as evenly as possible, with your knife.

15. Round every piece between two cuts, by twisting it carefully between your fingers.

16. Wet the inside of your circle and stick the lion's head nicely in the middle.

24. Roll a long sausage from yellow fondant and stick this on one side of the body.

25. Make three teardrop shapes from brown rolled fondant and add them to the end of the tail.

26. Stick a stick at the top of the body and let it dry for at least one day. After drying, slide the head carefully over the stick.

. tip .

The body of this lion is suitable to use for a lot of different animals.

ANIMALS

OWL

LEVEL OF DIFFICULTY:

6. Then push the spherical modeling stick again into the place where the iris will be and fill this up this with orange.

7. Take the spherical modeling stick and push it into the iris to make the pupil. Fill this now with black.

8. Give both eyes two small white balls to mimic the light's reflection. Make one ball bigger than the other and make sure the balls sit in the same place in both eyes.

1. For the head, form a ball out of brown rolled fondant.

2. Roll a piece of skin-colored fondant (or any color of your choice). Make this into an oval shape and draw a line in the middle of the top with a knife.

3. Stick this on the head and press it firmly.

4. Now push in the eye sockets with the spherical modeling stick.

5. Fill those both of these with white.

9. For the beak, add a triangle of orange fondant, between the eyes.

10. Give each eye as thin a black eyebrow as possible. Use brown fondant to make the ears and blend them against the head.

11. Add some extra lines at the bottom of the head to make the owl extra cute.

12. Now start with the body or stop at this point. If you add little wings to the head, you already have a fully-fledged owl. It's more fun to make all kinds of different owls with little variations.

13. If you do want to make the body, form a ball out of brown fondant, but make this one slightly smaller than the head. If you want your owlet to come across as extra cute, you can achieve this by making the head just a little too big for the body.

14. Give the body a small wing on each side. Use the same color as the body and make a teardrop shape for each wing. Stick these wings on the body with the point upwards.

15. Now add a belly to the body.

16. Insert sticks into the body and let it dry.

17. Make three small balls for each leg out of orange rolled fondant and stick them against each other. Make sure the middle one is the largest and the two outer ones are equal in size. Add the feet when the figure is already on the cake. That way there is less chance of them breaking.

DOG

LEVEL OF DIFFICULTY:

1. Form a ball out of white rolled fondant for the head.

2. Form a white sphere again, but much smaller. Place it in the middle of the large ball, but do this a little more towards the top.

3. Now make a small triangle of black fondant and place it on top of the white sphere With a toothpick, make a stripe just under the nose.

4. For the mouth, make a cavity with your pointed modeling stick. Indicate on each side of the muzzle the corners of the mouth. Then fill the mouth with black fondant.

5. Roll a small sausage of white fondant and add this to the bottom of the mouth. Blend so this looks good.

6. Take some pink fondant and make it into a small ball; push the tip of the ball in the mouth. Draw a line with your toothpick in the middle.

7. For the dog's hair, roll different white fondant sausages and place them one after one just above the muzzle. Do this by taking the end between your fingers and rolling it randomly up a bit.

15. Now place one paw on each hind leg. Make sure they are placed deeper than the two front legs.

16. Now push two sticks into the body and let it dry.

17. Carefully place the head over the sticks.

18. Roll another piece of white fondant and make sure it has a triangle shape. Now place this between the head and the body. This will give the dog's chest more volume.

19. Draw some lines in this with your toothpick to mimic the fur and then make a collar with red rolled fondant.

20. Make the collar tag in the middle by using the spherical modeling stick and a ball of gray rolled fondant. Paint that with metallic silver spray.

8. Draw lines in the hair with a toothpick to make it more realistic.

9. For the ears, take some grey fondant and make two balls. Stick one of them on each side of the head. Make sure the ears sit under the hair.

10. For the body, form a cone of white rolled fondant.

11. Flatten the top of the cone a bit.

12. With your knife, make a cut in the middle and cut off a piece on both sides of the cone.

13. Now form a paw on both front legs and blend it well. Create the toes with a toothpick and fold lines just above the paw.

14. For both hind legs, shape two balls of gray rolled fondant and stick them to both sides of the body.

ANIMALS

CAT

LEVEL OF DIFFICULTY:

7. Mark the position of the corners of the mouth with your fingers.

8. For the nose, make two small balls of white fondant and place them between the corners of the mouth.

9. Now take another piece of white fondant, but press it completely flat. Stick this under the nose.

10. Blend the outsides well.

1. Shape orange fondant into a ball and make sure that the top is narrower than the bottom.

2. With your fingers, push in the eye sockets.

3. Hold the ball firmly between your fingers and make a pointy shape on both sides.

4. Now deepen the eye sockets. Then with the pointed modeling stick make a line from the inside to the outside of both eyes.

5. Since the eyes are closed, use the same color as for the face instead of white fondant for the eyes.

6. Push in both eyes, but not too deep. The edges must remain clearly visible.

17. Make two triangles out of orange fondant for the ears and place them on each side from the head. Blend this well against the head and make sure the tops of the ears are pointy.

18. Using the flat side of the modeling stick, insert gently into the ears to create more depth.

19. For the body start with the same color as the one for the nose (the belly and the neck are therefore not orange). Start with a cone, but then make the bottom narrower than the top. Also make sure that the top is smaller and does not end in a point.

20. Make two sausages from orange fondant and add one on each side of the body. Make sure that they are narrower at the top.

21. Cover the entire back with a large rolled out piece of orange fondant and spread it over the back.

11. Now make a ball of red or pink fondant. Push the tip of it under the nose and add a line with the help of a toothpick.

12. Now take a piece of orange fondant and stick this just above the nose. Blend this in nicely.

13. To finish the nose, mix some red with brown fondant. Make a heart shape and stick this on the end of the nose.

14. Draw a line with a toothpick for the nose and give the cat nostrils by using the pointed modeling stick.

15. At the bottom of both eyes, add a small black line. Do this as thinly as possible.

16. Recreate the hair structure with a toothpick afterwards. Draw random lines everywhere.

29. Roll out an elongated piece in the same color as the neck. Paste this between the head and the body and blend it in well.

30. Using the toothpick, draw fine lines around the mimic hair texture.

31. Now take red or a color of your choice and make a thin collar.

32. Roll brown fondant into two balls for the medallion on the collar: a small one and a slightly larger one. Place the little one at the top and then stick the larger ball. Paint this gold.

33. Finally using a light color fondant, add different dashes and details. You can also do this with paint or by dusting. If you do it with rolled fondant, try to make it as thin as possible and to blend it out beautifully every time. Give these some 'hair structure' with your toothpick as well.

22. For the legs; add an orange ball on each side of the body. Push this well against the bottom of the body so that the top has more sticking out. These will be the two hind legs of the cat.

23. Now add four white paws.

24. Give each paw toes with a toothpick.

25. Using your toothpick, draw fine lines on each leg to mimic hair texture.

26. Now roll several long orange fondant sausages for the tail ending in a point. I placed three together but feel free to add another one for a thicker tail.

27. Push two sticks into the top of the body and let it dry.

28. Carefully place the head over both sticks.

PANDA

LEVEL OF DIFFICULTY:

6. With the pointed modeling stick push just next to the mouth to indicate the corners of the mouth.

7. Place a white ball in each eye.

8. Push the opening for the pupil with the spherical modeling stick and place a black ball in each eye.

9. Form two slightly larger black ones for the ears. Stick an ear on each side and blend this nicely on the head.

10. Give both eyes a small white dot to mimic light reflection.

1. Form a ball of white rolled fondant for the head. Push the eye sockets in with your fingers.

2. Fill both eye sockets with black rolled fondant. Press this in nicely with the spherical modeling stick.

3. Form a small ball of white fondant and place this between the eyes.

4. Now make the nose by placing a heart-shaped piece of black fondant between the eyes.

5. Draw a line with a toothpick in the center down from the nose. Then draw the mouth.

12. Using white rolled fondant, shape the body into a triangle.

13. Roll out a piece of black fondant and cover the top of the body.

14. Roll black fondant into two long sausages for the hind legs and feet.

15. Push up the ends of the sausages on one side with your fingers and make them a bit rounder. Mark the heels of the feet with the pointed modeling stick.

16. Stick the inside of the hind legs against the body.

17. Now use black fondant to roll out two drop-shaped sausages for the front legs. The thickest ends will become the paws. With a knife cut the line for the thumbs. Note: the thumbs point to the body.

18. Stretch the thumbs and make them rounder.

19. Stick the arms in place. Blend the top of both arms.

20. Stick a stick into the body and let it dry. After drying, carefully slide the head over the stick.

ANIMALS

FISH

LEVEL OF DIFFICULTY:

7. Blend this out as nicely as possible with the flat side of the modeling stick.

8. Use a toothpick to mark lines in both tail fins.

9. Add white rolled fondant to both eyes.

10. Mark the mouth with a toothpick.

11. Stick a small piece of yellow fondant against the mouth making sure it's the same length.

12. Blend this out nicely.

 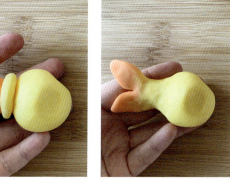

1. Shape the yellow fondant into a ball.

2. Push in the eye sockets, on both sides, with your fingers.

3. Stick a toothpick where the tail will be attached. Do use a toothpick here instead of the usual stick (the tail should be as thin as possible).

4. Use orange fondant to make a kind of heart shape.

5. Push this over the toothpick.

6. Shape the yellow fondant into a sausage and paste this between the tail and the body of the fish.

13. Pierce a hole in each eye with the spherical modeling stick. Fill this up with green. Prick another hole in it and fill it with black.

14. Give both eyes a small white dot, to mimic light reflection.

15. Add a small piece of yellow rolled fondant above both eyes.

16. Using a toothpick, mark a line under each eye and add a fin on both sides.

17. Now make the biggest fin in a sort of triangle shape with orange fondant. Paste this on the top of the head and blend it out.

18. Draw lines here too with your toothpick.

19. Finally, I added white balls with white rolled fondant here and there to indicate the water. This can also be done with blue, but I usually do it with white because it looks better on a blue cake.

CAKE DECORATIONS

65

PENGUIN

LEVEL OF DIFFICULTY :

1. Shape black fondant into a pear shape.

2. Now roll out a piece of white fondant and make this about the same shape, but slightly smaller and flatter. Cut a line at the top with your knife. NOTE: Black fondant usually leaves stains on your hands. So make sure to wash your hands after handling black fondant, especially before you use your hands to roll out white.

3. Stick the white fondant shape on the body and push it down well. Emphasize the separation between the head and the body by pushing the fondant under the head a little deeper.

4. Add a little bit of orange just below the cut.

5. Use the pointed modeling stick to prick a hole just below the orange ball.

6. At the bottom of the hole, add some more orange.

7. With the spherical modeling stick, push one eye in. Fill this with black.

8. Make the other eye on the other side a black half-moon shape.

9. Make an eyebrow with black on both sides and stick it on top of the white part.

10. Give one eye two small white dots to mimic light reflection, make sure they are different sizes.

11. Stick a small ball of pink fondant for the cheeks on both sides. You can also choose to dust, but I want to show you this way. As dusting doesn't always look nice with some figures.

12. Now add one of the wings by adding a triangle of black rolled fondant on the outside. Blend it well against the body.

13. Repeat again for the inside, but with white fondant.

14. Repeat steps 12 and 13 for the other wing.

15. Make two legs with orange fondant and stick them to the bottom of the penguin.

16. The penguin is now ready. If you want to make sure that he will stand firmly on the cake, you can always put a stick at the bottom of the penguin and push it into the cake. Leave the penguin to dry at least a day so you don't deform it when you put the stick in it.

. tip .

If you want to have multiple copies of the same animal, good to make each animal a bit different. Be creative with the animals and don't make identical ones. You can also play to your heart's content with the facial expressions (see p. 26). Be original and creative!

chapter

04

WELL-KNOWN CHARACTERS

BUMBA

LEVEL OF DIFFICULTY:

5. For the eyes, stick a small black ball on each side of the nose.

6. Roll black fondant between your fingers to form two very small fine sausages and stick them neatly above both eyes. Try to make them as level as possible.

7. Roll a fine black rolled fondant sausage for the mouth. Stick this just under the nose. Add a small piece red rolled fondant to the middle of the mouth to create the illusion that his mouth is open.

8. Give this red ball a small black line. Make sure it fits nicely on the mouth.

1. Form a ball for the head out of skin-colored fondant.

2. Make two skin-colored balls for the ears. These must be a lot smaller than the head. Make the ears as even as possible and stick them just below the centerline.

3. Blend both ears nicely against the side of the head.

4. For the nose, you form a ball out of red rolled fondant. Stick this in the middle, slightly higher than the ears. Do not push the ball too much; this will make it too flat.

14. Use your toothpick to make extra pleat lines on both sides of the body.

15. Add two arms at the top of the body. Be sure not to make them too long. Add some extra pleat lines here as well by using your toothpick.

16. Make a heart out of red rolled fondant and stick this in the middle of the body.

17. Make hands from skin-colored fondant. Form two balls for this. Use your fingers to flatten each ball and then make four incisions with a knife. Leave the thumbs pointing towards the body. Now stick the tops of the hands against the arms.

18. Now make the shoe that appears under Bumba's dress. Roll some black fondant in an oval and stick it against the body. Make an incision to indicate the heel.

9. For the hat, make a big triangle out of yellow fondant. Make the bottom of the hat a little bit wet and stick it in the middle on the head. Make sure the top of the hat is not too pointy.

10. Give the hat two red dots. The upper ball should be slightly smaller than the bottom one.

11. For the hair, make a number of small teardrop-shaped pieces out of black rolled fondant. One by one, paste four or five to the head. Blend this in the middle with the pointed modeling stick so that the hair of Bumba seems to form a whole.

12. Make a cone for the body out of yellow fondant and use the head as a benchmark or make sure the ratio of the body fits the head.

13. Push the cone against your work surface, to make the bottom more flat. Push one side of the cone up with your thumb and go over the fold lines with your pointed modeling stick.

UNICORN

LEVEL OF DIFFICULTY:

5. Place a small sausage out of white fondant just below the center of the nose.

6. For the eyes, use the pointed modeling stick to draw half a circle on each side of the nose to the outside of the face.

7. Repeat this just a little further up, but use a toothpick this time, to create some extra detail on the eyes in the form of a smile line. Also draw an extra pleated line just above the nose.

8. Mark the eyebrows with the flat side of the modeling stick.

1. For the head form a ball out of white rolled fondant.

2. Using your fingers, push the ball in a little above the middle and also push in the eye sockets.

3. Form a smaller white sphere and stick it on the place of the nose. Blend this nicely and give the unicorn some nostrils by pushing softly with the pointed modeling stick.

4. Press the flat side of the pointed modeling stick into the corners on both sides of the nose to create the mouth.

15. Just randomly continue rolling around the pink sausages until you are satisfied.

16. For the body, form a cone out of white rolled fondant.

17. With a knife, make a small line in the middle on the bottom and two slanting, longer lines leading to the outer edges for the legs.

18. Lightly soften the lines with the pointed modeling stick.

19. With your fingers, push the outer legs slightly more to the side, so that the two front legs clearly come to the foreground.

9. Roll some black fondant into two fine thin lines and place them on the bottom of the eyes. Tuck the top of your lines upwards. Repeat for the eyebrows.

10. Add extra eyelashes with black fondant, or with an edible black marker, if desired.

11. For the ears, make two small triangles out of white rolled fondant, and paste them in place. Blend them well against the head and give them some depth by pushing in the rolled fondant inside each ear.

12. Now make the horn (see Basic figures p. 37).

13. Now make different sausages from pink fondant and make sure that each sausage has a nice pointy end.

14. Roll the first sausage around the horn.

20. For the hooves, make two small flat pieces out of brown fondant and stick them to the bottom of the two front legs. Make sure that the line in the middle remains intact.

21. Now give the two hind legs a hoof. Make sure these stay behind the two front legs.

22. Make long pink sausages for the tail from pink fondant, just like you did for the mane. Make sure that each sausage ends in a point and align the sausages from the back of the body to the front side. Add as many sausages as you want. The number of sausages will affect the thickness of the tail. Draw extra lines in the tail with a toothpick to imitate the hair structure.

23. Stick two sticks into the body and leave at least one day to dry. After drying, carefully slide the head over the sticks.

FAT UNICORN

LEVEL OF DIFFICULTY :

6. Push in the eyes with the spherical modeling stick.

7. Push in the eyebrows with the pointed modeling stick. These point downwards this time.

8. Now push in the nostrils.

9. Fill the eyes with white and push a cavity for the iris with the spherical modeling stick. Fill this in with light blue fondant and repeat for the pupil. Fill the pupil with black rolled fondant.

10. Using a toothpick, very gently trace stripes in the colored part of the eye.

1. Form a ball out of white fondant for the head. Push the middle part in deeper with your fingers.

2. Then push in the eye sockets.

3. For the nose, add a small ball of white rolled fondant.

4. For the mouth at the bottom of the nose, add a small white piece.

5. Push in the corners of the mouth with the pointed modeling stick.

11. Give both eyes two little balls of white fondant for the light reflection. You make one a bit smaller than the other. For the eyebrows, add two fine brown stripes.

12. Flatten a small piece of pink rolled fondant between your fingers and stick it between the nose and the mouth. Draw a line in the middle and curl the tongue upwards around your modeling stick.

13. Now draw a thin black line above both eyes. Curl the outside of the line upwards. Use fondant or a black edible marker to add some extra lashes.

14. Now make the horn (see p. 38).

15. Make an ear on one side of the head. On the other side of the head comes the mane, so the second ear won't be visible.

16. Roll out several pink fondant sausages, ending in a point.

17. Start by wrapping the first one around the horn and work your way up as much as you want.

18. Form a kind of cone shape for the body, but make sure it slopes to one side and that the bottom is more of a spherical shape.

21. Create the hind legs in one piece. Push the thighs firmly against the body and blend well into the buttocks.

22. Now make four flat circles of brown fondant. Stick these against the bottom of the four legs.

23. Now give all hooves an edge and blend it so the ends look good too. Paint them gold later.

24. Roll two small sausages of the same pink rolled fondant as the mane and drape them over a leg.

25. Stick two sticks into the top of the body and leave to dry. When dry, carefully slide the head over the two sticks. If desired add some extra curls on the neck in pink rolled fondant.

19. Draw a line with the pointed modeling stick to form the bulge of the belly. Also give it a belly button.

20. Make two front legs that are reasonably thin on top and getting wider towards the hooves. Rest one of those front legs on the stomach.

CAKE DECORATIONS

79

SMURF

LEVEL OF DIFFICULTY:

1. For the head: make a ball out of blue fondant.

2. At the place where the eyes should be, push the ball flatter.

3. Push the two eye sockets with the spherical modelling stick. One eye socket can be a bit bigger than the other.

4. Now fill up the eyes with a white fondant. Don't push the eyes too deep: it is okay for them to stick out a little bit.

5. For the nose, make a ball out of blue fondant. Stick the ball between the eyes. Make sure to let the tip of the nose bend slightly to the right, just under the eye, as this creates the profile effect.

6. Blend out the nose, so you no longer see any lines.

7. With a toothpick, very gently draw the mouth on the face.

8. Make the smile softer by smoothing it with the flat side of your pointy modelling. At the same time, push in the corner of the mouth.

16. Stick two blue eyebrows above the eyes at the rim of the hat. Add a separate little black line at the top of both eyebrows.

17. Add a little piece of red fondant in the mouth.

18. Make a cone shape out of blue fondant for the body.

19. Unroll a long white piece of fondant and wrap it around the bottom of the body.

20. Push two little sticks in the bottom of the body in the space for the legs.

9. Push a little hole in the middle of the mouth. Do this in the eyes too. Fill the eyes with black fondant.

10. For the ears form two little blue fondant balls and stick one to each the side of the head.

11. Make sure to blend them in well and use a toothpick for creating details in both ears.

12. Stick a big enough piece of white fondant at the top of the head. Make sure it comes up high enough, as the hat has a little dip at the top.

13. Use a knife to make a line in the hat and with your fingers shape the top of the hat to a more rounded form.

14. Using the pointy modelling stick, push the hat evenly in the corners and make sure the hat connects neatly to the head.

15. Add an extra edge to the bottom of the hat and blend it in nicely.

21. Create both legs and feet in one piece, as they have the same white color. Slide each of them carefully over one of the sticks. The feet are allowed to be on the bigger side.

22. Now make two blue arms and stick them to the body. Make sure to make them slightly thinner towards the top of the body.

23. Put a little stick at the top of the body and let it dry for at least one day. After drying, you can gently put the head over the stick on top of the body.

DINOSAUR

LEVEL OF DIFFICULTY:

6. Fill both eye sockets with a ball of white rolled fondant.

7. Add green rolled fondant made into two small sausages above the eyes.

8. Push the eyes in with the spherical modeling stick.

9. Also add green rolled fondant made into two small sausages under the eyes. Curl them nicely around the eyeballs.

10. Fill the eyes with red rolled fondant for an extra scary effect. This can also be done with a different color of your choice.

11. Push in both pupils and fill them up with black fondant.

12. Add a thin black line above both eyes as well.

13. Give both eyes a small white dot to mimic light reflection

1. Form a ball from green rolled fondant for the head.

2. Shape the bottom of the ball to a point with your fingers. Flatten the top and stretch it up a bit.

3. Draw a line with the pointed modeling stick from the tip of the ball to the center.

4. Push in the corner of the mouth at the top of this line.

5. Push the eye sockets in with the pointed modeling stick.

19. Stick a thin strip of beige fondant along the front of his body. (Beige rolled fondant can be obtained by mixing brown and white fondant.)

20. Draw a few lines evenly with your toothpick.

21. Also do this randomly in the green section.

22. Add some spots here as well.

23. Using green rolled fondant make another cone shape for the tail, but make the tip very narrow and let it bend down a bit.

14. Push in the nostrils with the pointed modeling stick. Make them end in a point.

15. Draw extra fold lines in the nose and add an extra edge above both nostrils. Blend this, so it looks good.

16. Add some spots to your liking.

17. Give the dinosaur three small teeth.

18. We're going to cut the body into pieces. This is a nice option for figures that are very large or long. This way you can spread your figurine over different layers if you make a stack cake. Our dinosaur consists of two loose pieces, the body and tail, but a dinosaur or dragon can also be made out of more than two pieces. Shape green fondant into a long cone shape.

CAKE DECORATIONS

85

24. Add those same spots here.

25. We are now going to make leaves to create the illusion that the bottom runs even further down. So using fondant in another shade of green, make droplets and flatten them between your fingers.

26. Create a pattern in the leaves with your toothpick. Start from the center and then draw different lines outwards.

27. Now stick different leaves at the bottom of the body and tail. Stick a stick in the body and let it dry.

CAKE DECORATIONS

87

BABY

LEVEL OF DIFFICULTY:

This figure is ideal to decorate a cake for a birth, a baptism or a first birthday!

4. Push the eye sockets deeper with the spherical modeling stick and stick a small ball of skin-colored fondant in between for the nose.

5. Use a toothpick to draw a line under the nose for the upper lip.

6. Carefully enlarge the opening in the middle with the pointed modeling stick. Immediately push in each corner of the mouth.

7. Fill the mouth with black rolled fondant. Join the tongue to the middle of the mouth with red fondant.

8. Roll a piece of skin-colored fondant in a tear-drop shape and place it under the upper lip for the lower lip. Blend it well against the mouth.

1. For the head roll a ball from a piece of skin-colored fondant.

2. Push the eye sockets in with your fingers. (Since the baby is looking up, the eyes may be placed slightly higher.)

3. Roll two small balls out of a piece of skin-colored fondant for the ears. Paste an ear on each side of the head and with the pointed modeling stick blend them so it looks good against the head.

is important. A baby that is too big will look less cute. Use the head as a reference point to determine the correct ratio.

13. Roll a long rectangle from a piece of white fondant for the diaper. Make sure the diaper is slightly wider in the middle.

14. Wrap the diaper around the bottom of the body. Use a toothpick to make some lines in the diaper to mimic the folds.

15. Roll two long sausages from skin-colored fondant for the arms. Fold the sausages at the bottom for the hands.

16. Draw three lines in each hand with a knife to create the fingers. Fold the thumbs a bit beyond the other fingers.

9. Fill the eyes with some little white fondant and make a cavity for the iris with the round modeling stick. Fill it up with light blue fondant and repeat for the pupil. Fill the pupil with black rolled fondant. Give both eyes a small white ball of fondant to mimic light reflection. Make sure the one white ball is slightly larger than the other.

10. Make a small rectangle from a piece of white fondant for the tooth. Paste the tooth in the upper half of mouth.

11. Roll a piece of black fondant between your fingers to make it as thin as possible line. Place this on the line of the eyebrows. You can also do this with an edible black marker if you find that easier.

12. For the baby's body, roll a large cone from a piece of skin-colored fondant. The size of the cone

17. Place both arms on the body.

18. Stick a toothpick or stick into both sides from the diaper where the legs will go.

19. Roll two sausages from a piece of skin-colored rolled fondant. Fold the sausages in half for the legs. Carefully slide the legs over the toothpicks.

20. Roll two elongated balls from a piece of skin-colored fondant for the feet. Push the balls a bit flatter.

21. Stick a foot on each leg.

22. Roll eight small balls from a piece of skin-colored fondant for the toes. Make the two balls for the big toe a bit thicker and stick one on the top of each foot. Paste the other balls next to it.

23. Stick a stick at the top of the body and let it dry for at least one day. After drying, slide the head carefully over the stick.

CAKE DECORATIONS

PARDOES

LEVEL OF DIFFICULTY:

5. Use your fingers to push in the two eye sockets. Then with the spherical modelling stick push a smaller place for the eyes. You can also use your fingers to push in the corners of the mouth. You can feel where that is just next to the half-moon shapes for the cheeks.

6. With a toothpick you can make a curly line between both corners of the mouth to create a smile.

7. Now use the pointy modeling stick and push the mouth more open at the bottom. Use the same modeling stick to accentuate the lips. Also push in the corners of the mouth even deeper and make a line on each side.

1. For the head: make a ball out of red fondant. Push the bottom a bit in with your fingers.

2. Use skin-colored fondant to make three half-moons for the nose and the cheeks. Place these on the bottom half of the ball.

3. Take another piece of skin-colored fondant and make a ball. Flatten this between your fingers to about half a centimeter thick. Make sure it is almost as big as the red ball, just make sure it is slightly smaller at the top. Push a cut in the middle at the top using the spherical modeling stick.

4. Now place this part on top of the red ball and go over all the shapes of the nose and cheeks. Make sure to press firmly.

12. Use white fondant to form two small half-moon shapes; push these carefully in the mouth. A tip is to start with the teeth on top.

13. Form two more small half-moon shapes but out of skin-colored fondant this time and place these above the eyes. For the lash lines make a very tiny tin sausage out of black fondant.

14. Make two sausages for the lips out of pink fondant. Start with the upper lip, which also has to be a bit thinner than the bottom lip. Make sure to press it on very well, yet carefully, especially in the mouth corners.

15. With a toothpick you can make a line in the upper lip. Also make some fine lines in the bottom lip for detail.

16. Stick two half toothpicks in the side of the head, let them point towards you.

8. Now use the pointy modeling stick to push the mouth more open towards the top. Draw a small line between the nose and the upper lip.

9. Take a small piece of skin-colored fondant to create the nose. Push in the nostrils with the pointy modeling stick.

10. Now fill up the eyes with a white fondant. Use the spherical modeling stick to push in the irises. Fill these with brown fondant and push again with the spherical modeling stick to create the pupils. These, together with the mouth, can be filled up with black fondant.

11. Give both eyes two small white balls to mimic the light's reflection. Make one ball bigger than the other and make sure the balls sit in the same place in both eyes.

21. Bend the tip of the head a little bit forward and draw some lines in it with a toothpick.

22. Form a little square out of blue fondant and place it at the bottom of the hat.

23. Now make a little sausage out of brown fondant and place it above the blue square on the hat.

24. Create another slightly bigger square out of blue fondant and make a dent in the middle. Place this on the hat and make sure to stick it securely.

17. Roll two cones out of red fondant. Push the bottom of these cones over the toothpicks. With the spherical modeling stick blend these cones nicely against the head. Bend the tops of the cones toward the head.

18. Use brown fondant to roll out two little balls and place one on each side to represent the bells. With a toothpick make a small line on each bell and a dot underneath.

19. Place a toothpick in the head where the hat will end up.

20. This time, use blue fondant to roll a cone. Push the bottom of the cone over the toothpick and blend the cone smoothly against the head.

25. Roll three sausages out of brown fondant and place them against each other to create the ribbon of the hat. Twist the sausages into a spiral and place it on the top of the head. Roll a little ball out of brown fondant and stick this on the top of the ribbon.

26. Paint all brown parts in gold and let the head dry for a day.

32. Form two triangles out of blue fondant and drape them around the shoulders. Let them meet in the middle. Give the cape some extra pleated lines.

33. Make a little ball out of brown fondant and put it where the cape comes together in the front.

34. Roll a big piece of blue fondant and place it over the back.

35. Paint all brown parts in gold. Stick two sticks into the top of the body and let it dry for at least a day.

36. After drying, place the head over the sticks on top of the body.

27. Make a sphere out of red fondant for the body. Make sure to push in the base of the sphere and bend the tip.

28. Give the body extra lines to accentuate it.

29. Add an arm to each side of the body in red fondant.

30. Roll two balls out of white fondant for the hands. Push the balls flat with your fingers and cut three incisions in them with a knife to create the fingers. Make sure the thumbs point toward the body. Paste the hands on the arms.

31. Form two little rectangles out of brown fondant. Now cut two triangles on one side, try to make sure they have the same shape.

CAKE DECORATIONS

chapter 05

FOOD CARTOONS

RAINBOW

LEVEL OF DIFFICULTY:

5. With the pointed modeling stick blend the white balls on both sides to form a whole.

6. Stick a toothpick into the bottom of each cloud and let it dry for at least one day. After drying, carefully place the rainbow on the cake.

1. Roll a long sausage from a piece of blue fondant. When making a rainbow we always start with the inner color. Make an arch with the sausage and slightly wet the top.

2. Repeat this step with the second color and then with all the following colors. Work like this a evenly as possible. Always make the top a little wet so that everything sticks together well.

3. Cut off the ends of the rainbow evenly.

4. Stick white balls of fondant on the ends of the rainbow to create clouds

CAKE DECORATIONS

ICE LOLLY

LEVEL OF DIFFICULTY:

5. Give the cheeks a small ball of darker pink of rolled fondant to mimic a blush. Place these little balls under each eye.

6. Stick half a toothpick in the place where the wooden stick comes from the ice lolly.

7. Make a rectangular shape for the stick from a piece of (light) brown fondant. Push this over the toothpick. Blend out nicely with the pointed modeling stick, so the brown rolled fondant looks good against the ice lolly.

8. With a toothpick create some light lines on the stick of the ice lolly for the veins of the wood. Please note, if the fondant is too dark, the veins are less visible.

1. Roll a ball out of pink fondant (other colors are also possible) and push the ball flat with your fingers, to make a rectangle. Cut the bottom of the ice lolly.

2. Push the eye sockets in with the spherical modeling stick. With a toothpick, mark a half-moon between the eye sockets.

3. Fill the eyes with black rolled fondant.

4. Give the eyes a small white ball of fondant to mimic light reflection. Make sure that the one white ball is slightly larger than the other.

RASPBERRY

LEVEL OF DIFFICULTY :

4. Push the eye in with the spherical modeling stick. Mark a line between the eye sockets with a toothpick.

5. Using the pointed modeling stick make the line slightly larger at the bottom so that it fits the shape of an open mouth.

6. Fill the eyes and mouth with black fondant.

7. Give both eyes two small white balls of fondant to mimic light reflection. Make sure that one white ball is slightly larger than the other.

8. Make a small rectangle out of a piece of white fondant for the tooth. Stick the tooth in the upper half of the mouth.

9. Now take green rolled fondant and make small teardrop shapes.

10. Finally stick different green teardrop shapes at the top of the raspberry to create the crown of the raspberry. Add as many as you wish.

1. Using cherry pink fondant, roll out a ball with a pointed top.

2. Roll out several small balls of dark pink rolled fondant and stick the first ball at the bottom of the big ball. Paste the following balls on the left and the right of the first one and repeat all the way round.

3. Stick balls on the bottom of the larger ball and work upwards. Paste the full raspberry and press well.

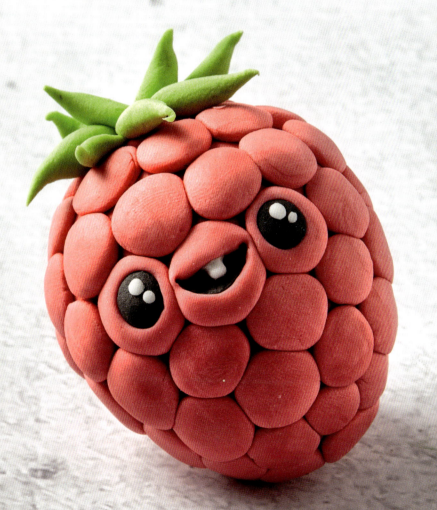

CAKE DECORATIONS

105

BLUEBERRY

LEVEL OF DIFFICULTY :

5. Fill the eyes with black rolled fondant.

6. Give the eyes a small white ball of fondant to mimic light reflection. Make sure that the one white ball is slightly larger than the other.

. tip .

As the berries are so small, it's always nicer to make several straight away. Give them different facial expressions, stack them on each other... Be creative!

1. Mix a piece of dark blue fondant with a small piece of red fondant to create a purple color. Roll a small ball out of this fondant.

2. Then use a small, sharp pair of scissors and start clipping. This will be the top of you berry.

3. With the spherical modeling stick, push in the eye sockets. Do this very carefully, to avoid distorting the berry by pressing too hard on the fondant.

4. Poke a hole with a toothpick in the place where the mouth goes.

CHOCOLATE CANDY

LEVEL OF DIFFICULTY :

6. Give both eyes a small white ball of fondant to mimic light reflection. Make sure that one white ball is slightly larger than the other.

7. Use a little light pink fondant on the cheeks to mimic a blush. Place these pink bubbles under the eyes. (The same effect can also be created by dusting, but this would be less noticeable due to the brown color of the chocolate candy.)

8. Roll a piece of light brown fondant (for this mix a piece of white fondant with brown rolled fondant) into a long sausage for the curl of the chocolate candy.

9. Make the top of the candy a little bit wet and wrap the sausage on it like a snail shell.

1. Roll a piece of brown rolled fondant into a blunt cone.

2. Push the eye sockets in with the spherical modeling stick.

3. Using a toothpick, draw a line under the eyes to create the mouth. Start under the eyes and mark an arc outwards on both sides.

4. Make this line softer by using the flat side of the pointed modeling stick against the bottom of the mouth. Push in the corners of the mouth straight away.

5. Fill the eyes with black rolled fondant.

APPLE

LEVEL OF DIFFICULTY :

6. Use a little dark pink fondant on the cheeks to mimic a blush. Place the bubbles under each eye. Place another dark pink ball of fondant in the mouth for the tongue. Draw a line in the middle of the tongue with a toothpick.

7. Give the eyes a small white ball of fondant to mimic light reflection. Make sure that the one white ball is slightly larger than the other. Make a droplet shape from a piece of white fondant and stick it on the top of the apple to mimic the shine.

1. Roll a ball out of red or green fondant. Push a cavity where the stem comes out.

2. Draw a line with the pointed modeling stick in the middle of the bottom.

3. Push the eye sockets in with the spherical modeling stick.

4. With a toothpick draw a line between the eye sockets. Use the pointed modeling stick to open the line in the middle.

5. Fill the eyes with black rolled fondant.

8. Stick half a toothpick in the cavity where the stem will be placed. Use a toothpick here instead of the usual stick as the stem must be fine and stay in place.

9. Roll out a small piece of brown fondant and make the top wider than the bottom.

10. Push the thinner side over the toothpick. Blend the brown fondant with the pointed modeling stick so that it fits nicely against the apple.

11. Make a teardrop shape for the leaf from a small piece of green fondant. Create the veins of the leaf with a toothpick.

12. Stick the leaf against the stem of the apple.

CAKE DECORATIONS

WATERMELON

LEVEL OF DIFFICULTY :

6. Roll a piece of green fondant into a thickness of 1 cm, cut out a rectangle from this.

7. Make the edge of the green rectangle a little bit wet and stick it against the white rectangle. Cut the excess green rolled fondant here as well along the outsides.

8. Make the openings for the eyes in the light pink fondant with the spherical modeling stick.

1. Since we are going to dust these well afterwards, we'll take some lighter colors for this watermelon compared to a real one.

2. Roll out a large piece of light pink fondant to a thickness of about 2 cm.

3. Cut out a triangle with a convex side.

4. Roll out a piece of white fondant with a thickness of 1 cm, cut out a rectangle from this.

5. Make the convex side of the pink triangle a bit wet and attach it to the white part, cut away the excess.

9. Use a toothpick to draw a line at the bottom of the eyes to create the mouth.

10. Carefully enlarge the line in the middle with the pointed modeling stick so it looks like a moon.

11. Fill the eyes and mouth with black rolled fondant. Don't push the eyes too deep; they may stick out a bit.

12. Make some small balls out of black sugar paste and shape them into teardrops for the seeds and stick them randomly on the light pink fondant.

13. Give both eyes a small white ball of fondant to mimic light reflection. Make sure that one white ball is slightly larger than the other.

14. Stick a small ball of rolled fondant in a darker pink shade at the bottom center of the mouth as the tongue. Mark a line in the tongue with a toothpick.

PEAR

LEVEL OF DIFFICULTY :

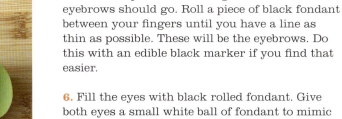

5. Place the pointed modeling stick where the eyebrows should go. Roll a piece of black fondant between your fingers until you have a line as thin as possible. These will be the eyebrows. Do this with an edible black marker if you find that easier.

6. Fill the eyes with black rolled fondant. Give both eyes a small white ball of fondant to mimic light reflection. Make sure that one white ball is slightly larger than the other.

1. Mix a piece of green fondant with a piece of yellow fondant. Roll out a large piece of this fondant in the shape of a pear. Make sure that the shape narrows at the top.

2. With the pointed modeling stick, draw a line in the bottom of the pear starting from the center.

3. Push in the eye sockets with the spherical modeling stick.

4. Create the mouth with a toothpick. Start under the eyes and work outwards.

7. Place a toothpick where the stem should go. Use a toothpick instead of the usual stick (the stem must be thin and stay well in place).

8. Roll out a small piece of brown fondant and make the top wider than the bottom.

9. Push this over the toothpick.

10. Make a teardrop shape for the leaf out of a small piece of dark green fondant. Create the veins of the leaf with a toothpick.

11. Stick the leaf against the stem of the pear.

CHERRIES

LEVEL OF DIFFICULTY:

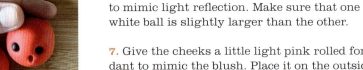

top left for the left cherry, and on the top right for the right cherry.

6. Give all four eyes a small ball of white fondant to mimic light reflection. Make sure that one white ball is slightly larger than the other.

7. Give the cheeks a little light pink rolled fondant to mimic the blush. Place it on the outside. The same effect can also be created by dusting, but this would be less noticeable because of the dark red color of the cherries.

1. Make two equal sized balls out of red fondant.

2. Push in the eye sockets with the spherical modeling stick.

3. Create the mouth with a toothpick. Start under the eyes and work outwards. The facial expression does not have to be the same with every cherry, you can choose anything.

4. Fill the eyes with black rolled fondant.

5. Give each cherry a long fine teardrop shape out of rolled white fondant for the light reflection on the cherries. Stick the teardrop shapes at the

8. Fold a piece of wire to form the stem. Push the brown rolled fondant over the wire, but leave a piece of wire uncovered at the bottom to push it into the cherries.

9. Carefully place the cherries on the stem. Blend the brown rolled fondant nicely against the cherries.

10. Make a teardrop shape for the leaf from a small piece of dark green rolled fondant. With a toothpick create the veins of the leaf.

11. Stick the leaf against the top of the stalk. Add as many leaves as you want.

ORANGE

LEVEL OF DIFFICULTY:

5. Fill the eyes with black rolled fondant.

6. Give both eyes a small ball out of white fondant to mimic light reflection. Make sure that one white ball is slightly larger than the other.

7. Push the spherical modeling stick over the entire surface of the orange to create the effect of the peel.

8. Make a stem with a few leaves like the pear (see p. 106) but make the stem for the orange a little longer.

1. Mix a piece of yellow fondant with a small piece of red fondant. Roll out a large ball out of this orange fondant.

2. Push in the eyes with the spherical modeling stick.

3. Create the mouth with a toothpick. Start under the eyes and work outwards.

4. For the bulging lip of orange fondant, roll a small sausage and stick it under the eye sockets. Blend the fondant nicely against the ball and with the flat side of the pointed modeling stick push it a little deeper into the corners of the mouth.

DONUT

LEVEL OF DIFFICULTY :

4. Push in the eye sockets with the spherical modeling stick. Create the mouth with a toothpick. Start between the eyes and work in a semicircle. Fill the eyes and mouth with black rolled fondant.

5. Give both eyes a small white ball of fondant to mimic light reflection. Make sure that one white ball is slightly larger than the other.

6. Roll small sausages in colors of your choice for the sprinkles on the donut. This time I used yellow and blue fondant. Stick the sausages on the pink fondant.

7. Give the cheeks a little piece of pink rolled fondant to mimic the blush. Place these under each eye. (The same effect can also be created by dusting.)

1. Mix a piece of white fondant together with a small piece of brown and a small piece of yellow fondant. Roll a large ball out of this dough-colored fondant and flatten the ball with your fingers.

2. Flatten a piece of light pink fondant with your fingers. (Or roll out the piece.) Cut the bottom in a wavy line, or push it into shape with your fingers. Place the light pink fondant on top of the donut and blend it in well.

3. With the spherical modeling stick, push a cavity in the center of the donut. Carefully make the cavity bigger with the spherical modeling stick.

CAKE DECORATIONS

119

HAMBURGER

LEVEL OF DIFFICULTY :

4. Poke small holes in the meat with the pointed modeling stick. Place the meat on the bottom half of the bun.

5. Flatten a few pieces of green fondant with your fingers for the lettuce leaves. Curl up the rolled fondant and place the pieces randomly on the hamburger meat.

6. Make a triangle out of a piece of yellow fondant for the slice of cheese and place it over the lettuce leaves. (The lettuce leaves and cheese are later covered by the top half of the hamburger bun, so this doesn't have to be that accurate.)

1. Roll a ball from a piece of dough-colored fondant (mix the rolled fondant the same way as for the donut on p. 118) and place the ball on a flat surface. Flatten the sphere with your fingers to mimic the bottom half of the hamburger bun.

2. Using a toothpick, draw lines along the side to mimic the texture of the dough.

3. Make a slightly larger slice from one piece of brown fondant for the hamburger meat.

to mimic light reflection. Make sure that the one white ball is slightly larger than the other.

14. Give the cheeks a little piece of pink rolled fondant to mimic the blush. Place these under each eye. (The same effect can also be created by dusting.)

15. Make some small teardrop shapes out of white fondant for the seeds on the bun. Stick the seeds on the top half of the hamburger bun.

7. Roll a long sausage from a piece of red fondant for the sauce. Drape the fondant between the lettuce and the cheese. Repeat with a piece of white fondant.

8. Roll a ball from a piece of dough-colored fondant for the top half of the hamburger bun and place the ball on a flat surface. Push the ball a little flatter with your fingers so that the bottom becomes nicely flat. Model the sides so that the bun will become more rounded at the top.

9. Using a toothpick, draw lines along the side to mimic the texture of the dough. Place the top half of the hamburger bun on top of the hamburger.

10. With the spherical modeling stick, push the eye sockets in. Using a toothpick, you create the mouth.

11. Using the flat side of the pointed modeling stick push each corner of the mouth in well.

12. Fill the eyes with black rolled fondant.

13. Give both eyes a small white ball of fondant

CUPCAKE

LEVEL OF DIFFICULTY :

4. Push in the eye sockets with the spherical modeling stick. Fill the eyes with black rolled fondant. Give both eyes a small white ball of fondant to mimic light reflection. Make sure that one white ball is slightly larger than the other. Poke a hole with a toothpick under the eyes to create the mouth.

5. Roll a long sausage out of pink fondant and let one side end in a point.

6. Make the top of the white cylinder a little bit wet and put the pink sausage on to it. Starting with the wider end, coil the sausage round like a snail shell, finishing with the pointed end.

1. Make a cylinder from a piece of white fondant for the bottom part of the cupcake.

2. Place the cylinder on a flat surface and flatten the top and bottom with your fingers. Make sure the top is narrower than the bottom. Then turn the cylinder over so that the narrower end is at the bottom.

3. With the pointed modeling stick, draw a line every half centimeter around the structure to imitate the cake. Then turn the cylinder over so that the wider end is at the bottom.

CAKE DECORATIONS

123

chapter 06

FESTIVE OCCASIONS

GIANT CUPCAKE

LEVEL OF DIFFICULTY:

A giant cupcake is, as the word implies, a large size cupcake. This one is mainly used for cake smash shoots, but can certainly serve as a birthday cake as well. For these photoshoots, we usually don't fill the giant cupcake. If this one is to eat, please do fill it.

tip.

Place the giant cupcake on a rotating cake stand to decorate it more easily!

1. Use sponge cake and buttercream for a giant cupcake. Do purchase a baking tin that already has the shape of a giant cupcake. This consists of a bottom and a top. Bake the sponge cake as usual and let it cool.

2. Cover a cake drum with rolled fondant and if desired, add a name to your cake drum.

3. Start with the bottom of the cupcake. Get it out of the mold. The lines of the baking pan should now be clearly seen on your sponge. Cut excess cake that has come over the baking tin and lightly grease the outside with butter (this is used to keep the fondant against the cupcake and you certainly don't need a lot of it). Roll out a long rectangle of fondant in a color of your choice. Do this somewhat thicker than usual; you don't want the cupcake visible through the fondant. If

you're doing this for the first time, your rectangle will most likely be too long and wide. This is no problem at all. The more you do this, the more you'll have the right dimensions. Mark vertical stripes in your rectangle using with the flat side of the modeling stick. Make sure the stripes are as even as possible.

4. Now hold the rectangle in front of your cupcake to check if your rectangle is too wide. If necessary, cut a piece off. It is better if the rolled fondant does not reach above the bottom part of the cupcake. Wrap the rectangle around the cupcake and let it meet at the back. Cut off any excess fondant. Take your pointed modeling stick and draw the vertical stripes back into the cupcake.

5. Now take the top of the cupcake. Remove it from the mold and cut off any excess sponge cake here as well. Place it on top of the cupcake.

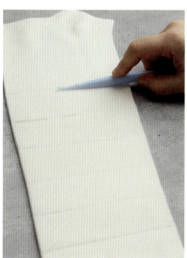

5. Make the buttercream in the color of your choice. Put this in a piping bag with a pointed nozzle. Ensure your buttercream doesn't curdle and stays firm by whipping it enough.

6. Now pipe the top part of the cupcake and start at the bottom of the back. Always pipe the roses starting from the heart. Try to do this as equally as possible. Work your way up and try to do this without holes in between the roses.

7. Finish with glitter or pearls if desired.

CAKE DECORATIONS

129

CHRISTMAS

LEVEL OF DIFFICULTY FIGURES: - CAKE:

This is my version of a Christmas cake. The figures are made for a special theme cake, but they can of course also be placed on a classic Christmas cake!

Santa Claus

3. Then take a toothpick and mark two lines under both eyes. One at the height of the jaw, and one a little higher.

4. Using the spherical modeling stick push in the eyes where the pupils should be. If your modeling stick is too thick for this, use the pointed modeling stick.

1. We start with the head. Shape skin-colored fondant into a ball and with your fingers push in the eye sockets. Also push in a little deeper next to the bridge of the nose.

2. Use a spherical modeling stick to push the openings for the eyes. For the nose put a ball in the place of the nose.

10. Make a slightly larger cone out of red rolled fondant for the body. You can keep the head next to it to determine the correct proportion for the body.

11. Place two toothpicks where the legs should come. If your toothpicks are too long, then break off a piece.

12. For the legs, place two cylindrical pieces of red fondant over the toothpicks on either side of the body. Blend the legs with the body so that they stick well.

13. Place an oblong piece of red fondant on the legs against the stomach. This will be the bottom part of Santa's coat. Blend this in well with the pointed modeling stick until you no longer see the join.

14. Then make the folds of the jacket around it more realistic by adding a white border.

15. Shape Santa's feet and use your toothpick to draw a line in both feet to indicate the heel. Give both feet a white edge.

5. Give your Santa a moustache and eyebrows out of white fondant. Mark lines in the moustache with a toothpick.

6. Now form two small balls of black fondant and press them into the eyes. Make sure that these spheres are as identical as possible. Give the pupils a small light reflection by adding a small ball of white rolled fondant. If it is difficult to hold this white ball on your finger, you can always put it on your toothpick and push it into place.

7. With the pointed modeling stick push a hole in the center of the moustache. This will be the opening of the mouth. Put a small black ball in it and then with skin color add a moon around the edge of the mouth to mimic the lip.

8. For the hat, form a small cone out of red rolled fondant and place it on the head. This cone serves to fill the hat. Take then a bigger piece of red and flatten it with your fingers. Now wrap this round the cone and blend it nicely out to the edges of the face.

9. Make the edge of the cap with white fondant. Gently poke holes with your toothpick to mimic the texture of the hat.

16. Roll two elongated sausages out of red fondant for the arms. Leave enough space between the arms to add hands.

17. Form two white balls for the hands. Flatten them a bit and make four incisions with a knife for the fingers. Always make sure that the thumbs are pointing towards the body. Give both hands a white border.

18. Stick toothpicks into the body and let it dry for at least one day.

19. If the body and head feel hard enough, put the head on to the toothpicks. Now add his beard of white rolled fondant and make some lines with the pointed modeling stick to accentuate the hair direction.

Gingerbread Man

1. Make a sphere of brown rolled fondant for the head. Make sure it is not too dark because the eyes are completely black, so then these would be hardly noticeable.

2. With the spherical modeling stick, push in the place for the eyes and place a flattened ball of red fondant between the eyes for the nose.

3. For the pupils, place a ball out of black rolled fondant in both eyes. Make sure not to push them in but rather let them fall in. This figure is even more beautiful if the pupil is the same size as the place you pushed in. That way, the eye will appear rounder. Then add a white ball for the illusion of light reflection.

4. For the mouth, carefully draw a line from one side to the other with your toothpick.

5. Make the mouth less sharp by blending the lower edge of the mouth with the pointed modeling stick.

6. Roll out a long thin strip of white fondant and put it carefully on top of the head. Push the strip gently with your fingers until you are satisfied it is in the right place. Let the head dry. Repeat these instructions for the back of the head and blend nicely along the points of contact.

Roll out the strips as thin as possible between your fingers and then drape them over the ends. Press the strips with the pointed modeling stick. Finally add the red buttons on the stomach. Make these a bit wet at the points where they should stick. Push them as little as possible so that they retain their spherical shape as much as possible.

13. Stick a stick at the top of the body and leave the body and head to dry for at least 1 day. Push the head carefully on the stick after drying.

. tip .

Since this is a very cute figure, it is important that the body is not too big in comparison to the head. Rather make the body a little too small than too big.

7. Then push a toothpick into the head at the point where the hat will go.

8. For the hat make two spheres out of white fondant, one is smaller than the other. Place the balls on top of each other so that the bottom part of the hat is smaller than the top. Push your toothpick into the top ball and create the pleat lines of the hat.

9. For the body, form a cone out of brown fondant, use the head to find the right proportion for it.

10. Push two toothpicks where the legs will be. This time make two legs with the feet already attached. So make sure that the ends of the legs are wider and bigger.

11. Add the arms to each side. Place the right arm between the legs so that it looks as if the gingerbread man is leaning on it. Paste the left arm behind the left leg.

12. On both the ends of the arms and on the ends of the feet add a long white strip rolled fondant.

Snowman

1. Shape a sphere for the head out of white rolled fondant.

2. Immediately add the eyes and mouth with small black balls (it is not necessary to push in the cavities first). For the nose shape a small cone out of orange fondant and place it between the eyes. With a toothpick lightly add some lines on the nose to make it look more like a carrot.

3. Then form two white spheres, one large and one slightly smaller. Let them dry and when everything is hard, place them on top of each other. For the large bottom ball, use a skewer. This is bigger than a toothpick and so you can place the three spheres together with one skewer.

4. Decorate your snowman however you like. I gave him some black buttons and a scarf. Let your imagination run wild.

Gifts

1. Make small packages in different shapes out of red fondant.

2. Then add a ribbon to each gift. Let your imagination run wild here as well.

Santa Claus's bag

1. You have two options for making this bag. You can either use a Styrofoam sphere inside or you can use a clear plastic ball. The advantage of using the plastic ball is that you can fill it with an extra surprise like cake or sweets for the kids. Styrofoam, on the other hand, is slightly easier to use with fondant coating, because it is not as slippery as plastic and bends slightly. Roll out a piece of red fondant and make this a little thicker than when you coat a cake. Cut a large circle from this.

2. Place the styrofoam sphere in the middle of your red circle and bring in all the outsides of this circle together at the top of the sphere. Push all rolled fondant together at the top so that you create the neck of the bag. Blend all the lines at the top nicely until you are satisfied. If necessary, draw on additional pleat lines with the pointed modelling stick.

3. Then take a white ribbon and tie it around the top of the bag. Make sure one of ends meest Santa's hands to create the illusion that Santa is holding it.

The cake

The edge of the cake itself is finished with meringue pieces. Dust both the figures and the cake to your liking. For the figures I used powder dye as usual. For the cake I used edible gel food coloring.

First cover the cake with orange fondant and draw a brick motif in it with the pointed modeling stick. Roll out white fondant and cut out of it a shape that should represent the snow. I have the edges of the white rolled toward the inside to make it look like the snow falling from the cake. Decorate the cake the way you like it and be creative! On the example I have added snow crystals with glitter and some snowballs.

EASTER

LEVEL OF DIFFICULTY CHICK: ★ ★ ★ - RABBIT: ★ - CAKE: ★

Celebrate Easter! Hide some chocolate eggs in the garden for the kids, decorate the house with a bunch of spring branches and surprise your family with this funny cake.

Chick

3. With the spherical modeling stick, make the openings for the eyes and draw a line between the bottom of the eyes.

4. Using the pointed modeling stick, draw the lines for the eyebrows above the eye sockets.

1. For the head, form a ball out of light yellow fondant.

2. Push in the eye sockets with your fingers and make the upper part of the head slightly narrower.

11. If necessary, draw light lines in the iris with a toothpick to give the iris some more depth. This makes the whole thing seem a bit more realistic.

12. Give both eyes a small round white dot to mimic light reflection.

13. For the body shape a cone out of light yellow fondant and push the bottom of it in the middle with your thumb.

14. With the pointed modeling stick, push a notch in the middle and then draw two lines in the form of an acute angle around the joint between thighs and body.

15. Stick a stick in each thigh where the legs will be.

5. Push your fingers between the eyebrows to create a small Mohawk.

6. Now push in the corners of the mouth with both fingers.

7. Place a small piece of orange fondant for the beak. Make sure the top forms an obtuse triangle.

8. Now use a toothpick to draw the line that defines the beak. Then repeat this at the top of the beak and give it two nostrils.

9. Fill the eye sockets with white fondant. After the white has been placed, use the pointed modeling stick again to push in the corners of the mouth so they come quite close to the eyes.

10. With the spherical modeling stick, make the cavities for the iris and then fill them in with green fondant. Then using the same stick make a smaller cavity in the iris for the pupil. Fill in the cavity with black.

23. Make a teardrop shape with yellow for the wings with a knife cut a few lines in the widest side to represent feathers.

24. Attach the wings by wetting them a bit and placing them at the top.

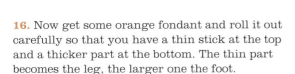

16. Now get some orange fondant and roll it out carefully so that you have a thin stick at the top and a thicker part at the bottom. The thin part becomes the leg, the larger one the foot.

17. Push the thicker piece a bit flatter with your fingers and then make two incisions. Emphasize the lines with the pointed modeling stick. Carefully place the top of the leg over the stick.

18. Draw some extra lines with a toothpick in the orange leg.

19. Place three little sticks at the top of the body and let the whole thing dry for at least one day.

20. Gently push the head over the sticks.

21. Take a piece of yellow fondant and stick it between the head and the body.

22. Blend this piece with the pointed modeling stick and then draw lines in it to mimic the feathers.

CAKE DECORATIONS

Rabbit

5. Roll another ball and place it in the middle. Squeeze this ball lightly with your fingers to mimic the fluffy tail. You could also create this with the pointed modeling stick.

6. Now place small pink balls on each paw, one larger one in the middle and three smaller ones above.

7. Roll out two long rectangles for the ears that end in a point. Stick a stick in the tip of each and let them dry.

8. Place the bunny's back end on the cake at a place of your choice and position the ears of the rabbit just in front of it.

The bunny is digging in the Easter cake and won't pop up with its head. So you only have to sculpt the rabbit's back end.

1. Shape a piece of white fondant into a large ball.

2. Form two equal teardrop pieces out of white fondant and with a knife cut the toes of the rabbit, each in a teardrop shape. These will be the paws.

3. Attach each paw to one side of the bottom and push the paws in the middle on each side a little so that the toes come a little bit more forward.

4. Now roll two small white balls and add one behind each foot to shape the folded leg.

The cake

This time we opted for a cake without rolled fondant. Which cake you make for the inside is completely up to you. For the outside I decorated this cake with KitKat cookies. I stick these against the outside of the cake with a thin layer of buttercream. To make sure that the KitKat fingers stay in place, I have tied them together with a colorful ribbon. To imitate the earth I used crumbled brownies. That mimics earth closely, but you can also go for a more colorful version. For example, you could use Smarties in the middle. For the grass I used buttercream with a gel dye colored green and used a pastry bag and a decorating tip to apply the buttercream grass to the cake and around the base.

HALLOWEEN

LEVEL OF DIFFICULTY FIGURES: ★ - CAKE: ★ ★ ★

3. Then use a toothpick to draw the line where the mouth will be. Start directly below the left eye and continue to the right.

4. Roll black fondant between your fingers making a line as thin as possible. Put this on the drawn line of the mouth and do the same for the eyebrows. You can also do this with an edible black pen if you find that easier.

5. Now place a small white triangle on each side of the mouth corners. Use a toothpick to put the teeth in position. If you want, you can add a small

1. Start with a basic shape with which you can make any face you want. Since it's about Dracula, start with white instead of skin-colored fondant. However, you are free to choose for yourself. Shape white fondant into a large ball and push the eye sockets in with your fingers. Make the openings for the eyes with the spherical modeling stick.

2. Now take two balls of black fondant and let each one fall into an eye. Try to make them both the exact same size.

drop of blood to the teeth as well. Give both eyes a small round white dot to mimic light reflection.

6. Roll a piece of black fondant for the hair. Make sure it's a triangular shape so that the hairline forms a kind of M. Make sure it fits well against the top of the head.

7. Form a cone for the body and with a knife make a cut in the middle of the bottom for the legs.

8. Make the two legs narrower with your fingers, so that they lose their sharp edges and let them point to each other.

9. Now poke a stick in the bottom of each leg so that later you can place Dracula on the cake.

10. For his shirt, roll a piece of white fondant, one that is large enough to cover the front. The cape will come over the back later. That way, you don't have to blend the shirt.

11. Draw some lines in the shirt with a toothpick to mimic its pleats.

12. Roll two arms out of white fondant and fix them on each side. Make sure they are narrower at the top than at the bottom.

13. For the cape, roll out a large piece of red fondant. Place the body on the rolled piece and cut the cape the size you want. Then fold it over the shoulders.

14. Now push a stick into the top of the body and let it dry. Slide the head onto the stick once the body is dry.

Little ghost

6. Now make two wings from white rolled fondant. Blend the wings where they meet the ghost so that they stick well to the body.

7. Carefully push a stick into the bottom of the ghost and let it dry.

1. Shape white fondant into a ball and pull the top and bottom to a point. Bend the tips to the left so that you get a moon shape.

2. With the spherical modeling stick, push in two eyes and fill one with black and one with white.

3. Under the white eye, apply a thin black line.

4. With a toothpick, mark the mouth just below the eyes and fill it with a black line just as with Dracula. Do the same for the eyebrows.

5. Using a small stick, make a mark on each side, level with the eyes, to show where the wings will go.

Mummy

1. For the head form a ball out of white rolled fondant.

2. Now form several white rectangles and wrap them over the head. Do this randomly; they can easily overlap.

3. Out of black rolled fondant make an eye, the mouth and a cross. These can all go on the same level and this time we're not going to press the rolled fondant first.

4. Make the body the same way as Dracula. Shape white fondant into a cone and using a knife make a cut for the legs in the middle of the bottom. Put a stick in both legs and make the arms the same way. Wrap a few strips of white around the body.

5. Stick a stick for the head at the top of the body and let it dry. Put the head on the stick when the body is dry.

Frankenstein

2. Push in two eye sockets with your fingers or with the spherical modeling stick and fill them with white.

3. Place a black ball in both eyes.

4. Now make two eyelids of the previously used green and stick them over each eye.

5. Now draw the mouth with a toothpick and let it hang down a bit.

6. Accentuate the corners of the mouth with the pointed modeling stick and make his lip on the bottom by adding a long sausage to his mouth. Blend this carefully along both corners of the mouth so that it the middle of the lip is thicker than the outsides.

1. For the head make a ball out of green rolled fondant, but push the bottom and top a bit to flatten it so it becomes more of a 'rounded rectangle'.

. *tip* .

If you want to dust Frankenstein later, please use a slightly lighter green than you would otherwise. This way the dust will look better later.

7. Give both eyes a small white dot to mimic light reflection and make the eyebrows. I added some above his eyes too. Add a bigger scar and a small one on both sides in grey to mimic the metal bolts on Frankenstein's neck.

8. Use the brown fondant to make a cone for the body and push the fondant out on both sides for the legs.

9. Put a stick in both legs and place a small piece of black over the sticks. Then shape the feet out of green fondant.

10. Add the details of the shirt with a toothpick by drawing light lines.

11. Push a stick into the top of the body and add one arm on either side. Make the fingers and toes with a toothpick. Let it dry. After drying, carefully slide the head over the stick.

Pumpkin

1. Form orange fondant into a ball the size of your choice.

2. Make five lines with a toothpick and try to draw these evenly.

3. With the spherical modeling stick, push in the top of the pumpkin and then add a small piece of brown fondant.

4. Blend the end of the brown over the pumpkin.

The cake

1. With this cake I started by hand painting the cake board. I covered it with light brown fondant. With the pointed modeling stick I drew lines in it to mimic the planks and then with a toothpick I drew the lines of the wood grains. After that I painted the whole board with brown gel dye and a little bit of water. You get more depth if you use multiple colors so feel free to include a little bit of yellow, red or gold to add extra accents.

2. I also painted the cake itself by using gel food coloring and a very small amount of water. Then I cut out some black fondant shapes to place both on the top and bottom of the cake.

3. The cake has two layers. So don't forget to use dowels!

4. The semicircle at the top is a smaller cake drum off which I cut a piece at the bottom and covered it with fondant. At the bottom I stuck three skewers in to keep it in its position.

5. Each layer is finished with brown sugar at the bottom. Use a spoon to place the brown sugar carefully where you want it. Try to use as little brown sugar as possible, since the cake itself is painted.

VALENTINES

LEVEL OF DIFFICULTY 2D FIGURE : ★ - CAKE : ★

2D painting is a great technique if you're interested in drawing and painting.

2D painting

. tip .

If you are not so good at drawing by hand, use tracing paper! Put your drawing on tracing paper and push the drawing into the fondant by going over it gently with a toothpick or a thin modeling stick.

1. Roll out a large piece of white fondant. Make it slightly thicker than when you want to cover a cake.

2. With an edible marker draw a picture of your choice by hand. This doesn't have to be perfect at all, at it is just to give you a guideline. After painting you can always put the final lines on it.

3. Now paint your drawing. Do this with as little water as possible. Water on sugar can form small holes or other damage, even if it hardens the fondant later. I usually use gel based paint.

4. If necessary, go over the lines again with a marker or with a brush with black paint.

5. Now cut out the drawing on the lines or leave a bit of white space around it.

6. Now dust a surface with icing sugar and put your drawing on it. Leave this to dry at least for two days. If you want to leave it upright on a cake, then prick it with a stick at the bottom before letting it dry. If you want your drawing to follow the curve of your cake instead of keeping it flat, then leave it to dry on a similar curvature (such as the bucket of your fondant). Make sure not to forget to dust your surface with icing sugar; otherwise your drawing will stick.

Cake

With this cake I placed the drawing on the side of the cake. You can do this by wetting the back of the drawing a little bit and wiping off excess icing sugar. Then I dusted around the drawings with pink. I finished the top with roses out of buttercream and fresh raspberries.

. tip .

Do the dusting before finishing the little string of balls at the bottom of the cake; because when dusting, some powder could easily fall on them.

MOTHER'S DAY

LEVEL OF DIFFICULTY BEAR: - CAKE:

5. Place a little bit of the beige fondant on both sides just above the jaw. Blend so it looks good.

6. With the pointed modeling stick, mark the place where the eyebrows should be.

7. Shape the ears out of beige fondant and blend them to fit well on the head. Shape the outer ear with the spherical modelling stick.

8. Make a nose out of a small ball of dark brown fondant. Make a kind of blunt triangle and mark the nostrils with the spherical modeling stick and the line of the nose with a toothpick.

1. Mix white fondant with a little bit of brown and yellow until you get some sort of yellowish beige. Shape this into a large ball for the head.

2. Push in the eye sockets slightly below the centerline of the head.

3. Now make two small balls out of white rolled fondant and place them just below the eyes for the jaws and one ball for the nose part.

4. Place a sausage of white fondant under the middle ball and blend the ends of this with the jaws.

14. Place these feet against the hind legs; if necessary, use a little water or a stick to stick them on.

15. Push a stick into the top of the body and leave it to dry. Because the arms are placed partly over the face, the arms are only done after the body has dried completely.

16. Once the head has hardened, place it carefully over the stick. Form the arms out of beige rolled fondant and cross them over each other. With a toothpick, draw a fold on each side of the arms to create the upper arm.

17. Take a piece of fondant in a color of your choice and make a long rectangle. Roll it up between your fingers. Paste the flower against the bear's jaw. Add some green fondant for the leaves and let the stem of the flower appear under the arm.

18. Add some details with a toothpick.

9. Fill the eyes with black and draw a line with a toothpick on the outside of each eye. Give both eyes two white balls to mimic light reflection. Make sure they are in the same place in both eyes and that one ball is larger than the other.

10. Add some extra fold lines with a toothpick to indicate the hair structure.

11. For the body of beige fondant, form a cone and make the lower part spherical. Accentuate the abdomen by drawing a line just above the belly. Place some white around the belly to emphasize it a little more. Blend this around the edges a little more so that the join is less sharp. If necessary, use a tiny bit of water.

12. For the hind legs, place a ball of beige fondant on each side of the body and then flatten them against the body. Blend these well against the body so that they stay in place.

13. For the feet, flatten two beige balls between your fingers and make an incision for the toes.

Place a white circle in the middle at the bottom of the feet. Fold the toes a bit over the white circle.

Cake

The cake is covered with pink fondant and the cake drum with pink fondant mixed with some white.

I put a circle of white rolled fondant in the middle and then you can write whatever text you like on it. On the internet you can find various free fonts. Write the word or name in the chosen font. You can always print the word on edible paper if you find that easier. Then place this circle on front of the cake and make the flowers. The purple flowers are more or less made the same way as the basic rose I used in the beginning of the book (p. 32), but this time you skip the flower bud and immediately start with the leaves. Make the ends of the petals fine by pressing them flat between your fingers and give each leaf a few lines. Then place the flower petal by petal on the cake. Push in the middle of each flower with the spherical modeling stick and then add small balls in the middle. You make the small white flowers with a cookie cutter. Usually I dust every flower, but this is entirely optional.

On top of the cake I placed some edible pearls and the cake is finished with a matching ribbon.

COMMUNION

LEVEL OF DIFFICULTY: ★ ★ - CAKE: ★

Little lamb

6. Accentuate the mouth by pushing the bottom deeper in with the pointed modeling stick. Also push the bottom of the eyes deeper. Draw a line around each side of the eye to indicate the jaw.

7. Place a white ball in both eye sockets.

8. Add a black line under both eyes.

9. Place an ear on each side of the head and blend them at the top into the face.

1. Form a ball for the head out of skin-colored rolled fondant, but make sure the top comes together slightly pointy.

2. Push in the eye sockets with your fingers.

3. For the nose, place a small piece of white rolled fondant in the middle under the eye sockets.

4. Then push the bottom of the nose into a more triangular shape.

5. Now draw the mouth with a toothpick. Start directly under the nose and then work outwards. Do this for the other side as well.

CAKE DECORATIONS

157

11. For the body, form a ball out of white rolled fondant. Push in two large cavities with your fingers and place at those spots white fondant for the two front legs. At the bottom of each leg, add a hoof made of skin-colored rolled fondant and draw a line in each one.

12. For the back hooves, push two skin color solid balls and draw a line in them. Make sure these two are behind the front legs.

13. Now cover the body with the wool, just the way you did it with the head.

14. Blend out the wool when you're done if you prefer that.

15. Place white fondant at the top of the body to form the neck and finish it by covering it with wool.

16. Carefully put two sticks in the neck and let it dry. Place the head on the sticks once the body is dry.

Cake

Three layers have been put on top of each other to stack this cake. So don't forget to put in dowels! The bottom layer is finished with roses made of pink sugar paste. For this I used the same technique as the basic roses (p. 32), I just placed them straight on the cake. First you put a teardrop shape somewhere on the cake, and then add the rose petals straight onto the cake as well. Please note that this is quite time consuming. I usually stack the layers first and finish off with the roses.

For the middle layer I have cut a label from white fondant and I then placed the name letter by letter on it by cutting out very thin strips each time. Then I used a very fine brush to paint the letters in gold.

10. For the lamb's wool make balls in different sizes out of white fondant and place them randomly on the top of the head. Start with the hairline first and work your way up until the whole head is covered.

The upper layer is decorated with drapes by cutting them the same way as for the text. Cut out thin strips of white rolled fondant and attach these to the cake piece by piece.

. tip .

Finish the bottom layer with a little bit of edible glitter and little pearls. This gives the cake that extra wow factor.

WWW.LANNOO.COM

Register on our website and we'll send you a newsletter to update you about new books and interesting personal offers.

Photography: Heikki Verdurme, Johan Blommaert, Tatyana Van Huffel (step by step pictures) and Shutterstock
Cover Image: Johan Blommaert
Graphic Design: Whitespray
Translation: Karen Van Huffel

D/2022/45/451
9789401486408

If there are any questions or comments: redactielifestyle@lannoo.com

All rights reserved. Nothing from this edition may be reproduced, recorded in an automated database and/or published in any form or in any way, whether electronic, mechanical or in any other manner without the prior written permission of the publisher.